Marmalade
&
WHISKEY

Marmalade
&
WHISKEY

British Remittance Men in the West

LEE OLSON

Fulcrum Publishing
Golden, Colorado

Copyright © 1993 Lee Olson

Cover design by Jody Chapel, Cover to Cover Design

Cover photo of William Drummond Stewart courtesy of Hastings House.
Cover photo of Brickwall Mansion in Sussex, England, boyhood home of
    Moreton Frewen courtesy of the Denver Public Library, Western
    History Department.
Cover photo of remittance men lined up at The Pines, with their host,
    Reginald Cusack (standing at center) from the collection of Mrs. James
    Jensen, Fowler, Colorado.

Library of Congress Cataloging-in-Publication Data
    Olson, Lee.
        Marmalade and whiskey : British remittance men in the West / Lee Olson.
            p.   cm.
        Includes bibliographical references and index.
        ISBN 1-55591-110-2 (pbk.)
        1. British Americans—West (U.S.)—Social life and customs. 2. British—
    West (U.S.)—Social life and customs. 3. Gentry—Great Britain—Social life
    and customs. 4. West (U.S.)—Social life and customs. I. Title.
    F596.3B7044   1993
    978'.00421—dc20   92–54762
                                                                            CIP

Printed in the United States of America

0 9 8 7 6 5 4 3 2 1

Fulcrum Publishing
350 Indiana Street, Suite 350
Golden, Colorado 80401-5093

Dedicated to the wise counsel of
Dr. Patrick A. Dunae,
the vivid recollections of Jack Ogilvy,
the sharp-penciled editing of Gail Pitts
and the unflagging support of my wife, Mary

Contents

Preface

This book's origins spring from my work as a reporter and editorial writer for *The Denver Post*. Probing the West's history and economics soon reveals the paper trail left by pioneering British adventurers—many of whom moved on to other places but left their mark on Western ranching, mining and culture.

Among these visitors were the remittance men who crisscrossed the world in the late nineteenth century. Their shadowy trails have inspired authors like James Michener and Hamlin Garland to explore their expatriate existence far from their British upper-class homes. The story is a fascinating one.

However, defining such "second sons" is a puzzling task because they present a moving target. Take the case of Lyulph Ogilvy, son of the eighth earl of Airlie in Scotland. Settled in Colorado by his family, Ogilvy spent his youth as the wildest kind of remittance man. He ranched and built irrigation ditches and raised general hell when he was in a bar. He killed a few horses in wild escapades with carriages and wagons and dissipated 300,000 dollars of family money before he went broke. As a reformed drunk he then became a farm writer for *The Denver Post*, which encouraged readers to call him "Lord" Ogilvy even though, as a younger son, he was untitled.

Ogilvy had more spunk than the average young Briton, yet a fellow *Post* writer, Joy Swift, wasn't fooled. "He was a remittance man," she recalls. "The *Post* didn't pay him much because he didn't do much. They were just using his aristocratic name." But she concedes his charm and fine sense of humor, which help explain why he has a separate chapter in this book.

Clement (Ben) Bengough, by contrast, was a lonesome remittance man who ranched in Wyoming, chased wolves and coyotes with Siberian wolfhounds and once wrestled a bear. But like Ogilvy he was a gentleman who didn't discuss personal affairs with outsiders. It was a trait that made them intriguing— even as it served as a barrier to learning what they were like.

Midway through the research an event in Britain lifted my spirits: a steeplechase horse named Remittance Man, foaled of Prince Regent and Mittens, emerged at the end of 1991 to become one of the greatest current British jumpers. I couldn't pass up the challenge. I put 70 pounds on him at Cheltenham. He won. I then bet 20 pounds on him at Liverpool. By that time he was so awesome (nine victories out of ten) that few horses were entered against him, so his winnings were slight.

I decided that, although many a remittance man faded in the backstretch (in my early research), don't bet against him. If really challenged he sometimes came home a winner.

Acknowledgments

I would like to thank the following people: Carol Shwayder, Dave and Sarah Weber, Joy Swift, Gwen Hayball, M. Ellen Hughes, Joe Barros, Irene McCormick, Jack Ogilvy, Charles Ian Finch-Knightley (eleventh earl of Aylesford), Raymond and Betty Cory, Phil Panum, Augie Mastroguiseppe, Mel Duncan, Ronald R. Kelso, Leeon and Doris Hayden, Helen Graham, Judy Wilner, Don Seawell, Florence Lister, Barbara Mackay, Robert Montague Kennedy, Sir Robert Cave-Browne-care (sixteenth baronet), Katie Kawamura, Dottie Ambler, Chuck Henning, Irene Francis, Jim and Kay Jensen, Eleanor Gehres, Reba Massey, Peggy Ford, W. D. Farr, Dan Escontrias, Harry Chrisman, Helen Mann, Betty Boston, Pauline Robertson, Montgomery H.W. Ritchie, Byron Price, Fred Russell, Claire R. Kuehn, H. Allen Anderson, Betty L. Bustos, Rachel Wikstrom, Joyce Culton, Bryant R. Dunn, Pat Mosch, Art Veysey, Gene Gressley, Jane and Bud Lowell, Bud Snidow, Frank Derrick, John Haig, Julia Gaisser, Margaret Kelley, Mel Duncan, Philip Kennedy, Elwyn Evans, Bob Tweedell, Judith Wright, Steve Frazee, John MacRitchie, Henny King, Francisco Azcarate, Joe McGowan, Ruth Marie Colville, Frieda Ruark, Virginia Sutherland, Esme Harcourt Williams, Fred Pruett, David Waddington, Earl Cress, Delbert True, Harold

Hagemeier, Kathy Price, Celesta Adams, Sandra Atchison, Ben and Elizabeth Kettle, Doris Porth, Rick Ewig, Noreen Riffe, Donny White, Mrs. Floyd Mays, George W. Woodard, Liston Leyendecker, David Twiston Davies, Margot Peters, James A. Little, Gene Levin, David Williamson, Gerald Phipps, G. Marvin Beeman, Ginny Kiefer, Mildred Wood, Jose Bustillos Delgado, Jorge Bustillos Delgado, Arturo Valensuela, Hayes Stripling, Dr. Arthur Q. Larson and the Marquess of Waterford.

Introduction

We had (in the 1880s) a colony of Englishmen, all educated, and with some money; I knew some of these were remittance men. I would hang around their cabin, and they would lend me books, and treat me with their food sent from England. Here I first saw chocolate, orange marmalade and Worcestershire sauce. These men always expected to strike it rich and lived from year to year on hope. ...

One of these, Butterfield ... once had over a million dollars, and spent it in France gambling. He lived among us for years ... but all at once he started to drink. ... He got lower and lower. ... Sickness came to him and he was sent away to die.

—Anne Ellis
Life of an Ordinary Woman

Such stories of lonely migrant Britons echo from remote and isolated places in the last century. Set apart by primogeniture (the exclusive right of inheritance of the eldest son), they left good homes with hope that money sent from home—in the form of family remittances—would help them achieve independence in developing lands. If they had a commonality it was that they were well-educated gentlemen who delighted too much in sport and whiskey and simpler pleasures remembered from boyhood, like Yorkshire pudding or marmalade. And too soon they got old.

Anne Ellis, writing of her childhood in the Colorado mining camp of Bonanza, captured them well. Some of her Britons were virtual hermits but still had a kind spot for the children of the frontier, glad to share with them small treasures or tell them of the great world beyond the horizon. And they were everywhere, having left England by the hundreds for Australia, Asia, Africa and America's western plains.

Children in a remote valley might find these lonely gentlemen fascinating but their parents were less charitable. From Perth, Australia, to Winnipeg, Canada, and points between— local settlers made a joke of the remittance men and their naïveté. Did one of them really try to round up jackrabbits with a flock of lambs? Did another try to harness a mule between the handles of a walking plow? The wildest tales, tinged with ridicule, were reserved for these drifters' drinking escapades. The arrival of their remittance check often meant that they—and their friends— would drink whiskey until the money was gone. They lived between two worlds: rejected by one and regarded as an undependable eccentrics by the other.

The term "remittance man" will be unfamiliar to many readers, but it was common at the turn of the century. Australians claim authorship of the phrase, but perhaps it's a moot point: The meaning varies with geography.

How remittance men evolved is explained in subsequent chapters. Put simply, their families held power in Britain through an aristocratic system based on primogeniture. The eldest son was pivotal: His succession kept the estate intact through laws he could not break. Only rarely could such land be sold. The system held firm for some eight hundred years—until the time of World War I—but it had an unfortunate byproduct: the younger sons who inherited no land and whose only recourse was to enter the professions or be sent overseas to seek opportunity. All too often the rainbow of overseas adventure led not to gold, but to futility interspersed by periodic remittance checks from home.

In Britain the phrase "remittance man" designated a younger son who was a "rotter" and an embarassment to his family. In the western United States, Canada and Australia the term was applied more casually. Any well-spoken, well-dressed young

Briton who received remittances and couldn't find steady work was quickly dubbed a remittance man.

But values changed rapidly as the century closed. Victorian morals gave way to understanding and forgiveness. The offenses that earlier caused wealthy families angrily to send the younger son abroad now seem mild. An editor of *Debrett's Peerage* (a venerated guidebook of the aristocracy) told the writer the sins meriting banishment in Victorian times were usually cases of "young people being young people—but not getting away with it."

The definition may never be clear. Jack Ogilvy, ninety, a retired University of Colorado English professor and son of one of Colorado's most interesting Britons, Lyulph Ogilvy, says firmly his father wasn't a remittance man because he was not "sent away."

Alexander Mackay-Smith, American author and scholarly historian in the field of horsemanship, is dismayed by simplistic labels. Asked if the young migrants were weaklings, he said, "Not at all. That's very unfair. A gentleman simply didn't engage in trade. They were gentlemen and their contributions were of a gentlemanly sort."

Dig beneath the superficial factions and one finds that these pleasure-seeking British adventurers contributed immensely to the intellectual and cultural life of the places they visited or settled in. They influenced architecture, style, manners and culture. The largest city in the Rocky Mountains, Phoenix, was named by Darell Duppa, a remittance man with a knowledge of the classics. He had many weaknesses, including drink, but in intellect he was a Socrates in a sea of frontier illiterates.

So today there is growing realization that families, especially in Canada and the American West where so many of remittance men settled, should take new pride in these ancestors, and as a start, they might review Rudyard Kipling's words on the subject.

Traveling in North America, Kipling took issue with Canadians who said remittance men were inept loafers. One oft-told story was repeated: of the lost remittance man found half-dead of thirst beside a river. When he was asked why he didn't drink, he said, "How the deuce can I without a glass?" Kipling returned the fire:

> All these are excellent reasons for bringing in the Englishman. It is true that in his own country he is taught to shirk work, because kind, silly people fall over each other to help, and debauch and amuse him. Here, General January will stiffen him up. Remittance men are an affliction … but your manners and morals can't be so tender as to suffer from a few thousand of them among your six millions.

Then he added, "Every new country needs—vitally needs—one-half of one percent of its population trained to die of thirst rather than drink out of their hands."

A subtle view but a wise one. A slightly different tack is taken by Canadian historian Gwen Hayball, who notes that remittance men unfortunately became synonymous with rich Englishmen. "Unfair," she says, as many men had a private income from home that had nothing to do with their dependence on their families. Further, she adds, the categories intertwine: "Since there are people who still like to recall memories of the so-called remittance men, it may not be too late to segregate the black sheep from the rest whose total remittances did, after all, help to swell the coffers of the country."

Some of them still are around, but as Gwen Hayball says, they have submerged in today's populations.

But let their stories speak for themselves. This was an interesting breed whose earmarks were a good education, gentlemanly manners, a little laziness and a thirst for whiskey. Oh, and marmalade. Bob Edwards, an irreverent Calgary journalist who made a parlor sport out of skewering remittance men, observed in the early 1900s:

> Just one more idiosyncrasy peculiar to the Englishman. … He cannot eat his breakfast without the adventitious aid of marmalade. Marmalade he must have … and your Englishman, no matter what part of the world he may be in, always insists on the bally waiter fetching some marmalade, don't you know.

Maybe marmalade was one of the few pleasures a remittance man pinched for money could still afford—that and (when the check came in) the whiskey which made his days in exile go a bit faster.

But let's not be too serious. These were men with, in the words of Canadian writer Ken Liddell, "a subtle and nimble British wit," illustrated by the story of the remittance man on an Alberta ranch who was asked by a newcomer the whereabouts of the lavatory. The remittance man surveyed the rolling range and with a wave of his hand replied, "Lavatory? Why, my good man, it's all lavatory."

✤
CHAPTER 1

The British Are Coming, the British Are Coming

If you could step back in time and take a coach ride through rural Britain in the 1870s, you would see a fairyland of quiet countryside, studded here and there by the great houses of the aristocracy and landed gentry. Beckoning distantly, these huge masonry piles, often white or beige, were gems mounted in green landscapes of oak, beech and chestnut amid manicured lawns and flowerbeds. Stretching beyond massive stone gatehouses, gracefully curving carriageways led visitors to the mansion door where a groomsman waited to take charge of the horses.

To arrive socially in the 1870s, of course, you would have had to belong to the right class. This was a time when a gentleman was defined in law as "a man who has no occupation." For at least five hundred years landed gentlemen were the British equivalent of the patricians of ancient Rome.

The further definition of a gentleman as "one who does not worry about money" wasn't precisely accurate, but between the two concepts lies great insight on the whole structure of aristocracy and landed gentry. How their property rights evolved determined what these landed families were.

One thing they were not: They were not members of a farm laboring class who had worked their way to success with calloused hands (unless you permit an exception for wielding a sword in battle).

What these gentlemen were is embedded in history. A great many families held the land simply because their ancestors had fought on the winning side in Britain's internal struggles, dating from 1066 when William the Conqueror rewarded his loyal Norman followers with grants of land and titles befitting a noble's standing as a landowner. The king seized the fortresses, controlled government and commanded the military. But land was where real strength lay and Britain's fair countryside soon fell as booty to William's loyal barons and their heirs. For centuries these ancient family crests—increasingly mixed with English and Celtic blood—held the land as the main producer of wealth through animal husbandry, cultivation and the human and animal power required to run it. It was also vital that a family's antecedents had married well and essential that its inheritance go to the eldest son.

Which raises an important question: What if you were not the eldest son? A younger son of a landed family was on a slippery slope where missteps were not forgiven. If you were such a younger son you watched your eldest brother go off to the best schools; the family was preparing him to succeed your father. That didn't rule out good schooling for you—perhaps even Eton and Oxford if you were bright enough. Further, the family would use money and influence to secure you an officer's commission or place you in the clergy or some other profession. But if you were slow getting started, inclined to be a fop or a troublemaker, out you went.

With varying degrees of pressure—often a gentle suggestion that "we want to help you get on your feet as a rancher in Canada or Texas"—you were made to understand that you were no longer welcome at home. The family would remit money to you overseas. The ninth definition of "remit" in Webster's dictionary is, "To transmit or send, especially to a distance, as money ... "

The emphasis was on distance. In worst-case scenarios the remittance money would be sent *only* to some far-off place such as Calgary, Vancouver, Sheridan, Cheyenne, Denver and San Antonio—or to Australia, India, South Africa and elsewhere.

These "second sons," as Britons themselves preferred to call them, often felt betrayed when they arrived overseas. Their opportunities had been much oversold and, worst of all, few had any training for the frontier. Many of them thus were lost in a cultural backwater and joined that strange broken brigade of adventurers who scattered through western Canada and the American West a century ago. Too proud to go home (and if they did, to what?), they made the best of life on the frontier, often waiting for the next remittance check.

What, then, were the conditioning forces that defined the remittance man in the 1870s when the outflow of younger sons really started? The answer begins with economic pressures that, both at home and abroad, were altering landed families' ancient ways of life, even though socially and politically they still sailed on like powerful ships through increasingly rough seas.

There were two kinds of families living on those beautiful country estates in the 1870s, as their forefathers had for many centuries. The division between the two types of families could be summed up as follows:

The aristocracy.
A joining of Greek words for "best" and "rule," the aristocracy was the landed nobility. There were only a few hundred such families, each headed by a father who, like his father, had been an elder son who had inherited the estate from his father, an elder son. They held hereditary titles like duke, marquess, baron and baronet. Their wives held the titles of duchess, marchionesss, baroness or lady. Aristocrats ranked just below royalty.

The landed gentry.
These families ranked beneath the aristocracy, but they numbered in the thousands, compared to the relative handful of aristocratic families. Their estates were inherited in the same way as the aristocracy. There was somewhat more mobility here: A rich industrialist could become a landed gentleman fairly easily by buying enough land and living like a country squire, whereas the hurdles to entering the aristocracy were many pegs higher. Landed gentry and aristocracy had one thing in common: They did not work with their hands or train their children to be anything but gentlefolk.

Great power—virtually all authority not claimed by the sovereign, the church and large municipalities—resided with these groups in the 1870s as it had for centuries. About four-fifths of the land of Great Britain was held by seven thousand families owning estates of at least one thousand acres; two hundred fifty families at the very top each had estates of more than thirty thousand.

These estates were kept intact through a system given the Latin word for "first birth"—*primogeniture*, the law of inheritance.

Originally, primogeniture was involved largely with physical protection. Designating a son, usually the eldest, as chief heir was common in ancient times. Although Roman law evolved to give daughters equal shares of a family's estate, a Roman general who had no sons sometimes willed land to a faithful officer on the latter's promise to protect his master's surviving family. In Europe in the Middle Ages primogeniture was common but gradually languished. But in Britain, primogeniture thrived, both as a guaranty of family survival and a tool of the state.

The system was tidy. It preordained a chain of command in battle or a response in community affairs that everyone could understand. If the castle was under siege and Lord Henry took an enemy arrow in the neck, every defender knew the line of succession: The eldest son would take command, or his regent if he were underage.

But the origins go deeper. In ancient Britain powerful regional lords kept groups of lesser nobles in thrall for purposes of collecting taxes and providing soldiery for regional uprisings or to serve the king in case of war. Their leverage was the five-hundred-year-old law of entail that reinforced primogeniture by forbidding any sale or whimsical disposition of estates that had been "entailed." Only Parliament could break an entail. The lord of the estate was entitled to its income while he lived, but he was bound to pass the property on to his eldest son or other male relative if he had no sons. Not all estate lands were entailed—and these could be sold—but most large properties were preserved through this ancient system. Protected from the splintering effects of equal inheritance, they remained unified, easy to tax and govern, with their resources accessible to higher authority.

This logic might be lost on a second son but other family members actually saw the system as enlightened. There were practical benefits in renting the estate's thousands of acres as units of a whole rather than dividing it among the heirs. Britons were aware of what had happened across the channel: Revolution had reduced French estates to ridiculous postage-stamp plots.

Primogeniture often was also undergirded additionally by *strict settlement* agreements between father and eldest son. These agreements specified that daughters would be encouraged to favorable marital alliances through active social life and a good dowry. The future family head also agreed to help his younger brothers' careers by buying them officer's commissions in a crack guards unit or using influence to secure church or government posts for them.

In the 1870s, however, opportunities dwindled. In 1872, the army stopped selling commissions and began choosing officers by merit test. Civil service followed suit. The clergy lost some of its gentlemanly appeal, partly because of low salaries. The worries for the head of the family thus increased as placement became more difficult. Another serious complication arose to add still another incentive for sending second sons overseas—changes in agriculture.

Britain was in the beginning years of a long rural depression resulting largely from New World productivity. Stimulated by Parliament's repeal of protectionist legislation, a brisk import trade sprang up with the arrival in British ports of great quantities of grain, fiber and live cattle from America and other areas of British influence. Some years later, when refrigeration ships plied the Atlantic, American beef exports increased dramatically. Adding to British farmers' troubles, deadly anthrax bacteria spread from the continent to their cattle herds, requiring greater dependency on beef imports, which reached an annual rate of thirty thousand tons by 1878.

Larger landowners escaped the downturn through sheer size or through coal wealth. Expanding industries needed coal and many estates had it. It could be mined at a handsome royalty. Others, unable to compete against the agricultural imports, sank into the ranks of the land poor. Even if land could be sold, entrenched families would not sell. Shifting their resources to improve profits in business or industry was unthinkable—beneath their station!

So they struggled on. And what had been an occasional oddity—the adventuring young gentleman going abroad at midcentury to explore strange lands and indulge his appetite for blood sports—now became commonplace as hundreds, even thousands, of younger sons were forced to go overseas to seek their fortunes.

Those dandies of the early part of the century had created admiration abroad as they dispensed pound notes for fun and high adventure. They really were upper class—poised, educated and maybe even wearing a medal for distinguished military service.

But by the 1870s the arrival of less-moneyed but still well-dressed Britons on the frontier in search of ranching profits was a bit ludicrous in American and Canadian eyes. The average newcomer was young and therefore a tenderfoot. And if western cowboys and settlers noticed he was getting money from home, he diminished further in their estimation, becoming in common parlance, a remittance man.

For such newcomers problems were virtually inborn. It was both amusing and tragic that the young Briton had been trained from boyhood *not* to be a hard-working Canadian or Wyoming or Texas rancher. He was upper class. Working with, say, a shovel, or even saddling a horse, was unthinkable.

The world was passing these young men by, but the halcyon days lingered delightfully for decades. Here is how you, as a second son, might have lived in the 1870s, even as your father's (or elder brother's) debts piled up alarmingly.

Aside from a few years at public school, much of your time would be devoted to sport and idleness. Arising late, you might want a bath, but you would not seek out a bathroom. A servant would come along with a portable tub, hot water and a screen so you could bathe in comfortable privacy before the well-stoked fireplace in your bedroom.

A canter after breakfast? Orders would go to the stables and a groomsman soon would bring up a saddled horse.

The kitchen would be well staffed. A local servant might be head cook, but if the family was of high standing, it very likely would pay handsome wages for a kitchen commanded by a French chef.

The farming would be done by tenants who gathered annually in the mansion's justice room to discuss cultivation agreements and to pay your father the rent for crop and livestock production. In effect, the lord or landed gentleman ruled a small kingdom that involved him in, besides farming, the administration of local laws and public services. Justice of the peace may seem a trivial title today, but in the 1870s such a title gave a landowner important duties and substantial regional prestige.

Servants and tenants together might range from fifty to several hundred, creating a need for housing, schools for the children and a chapel. For the ruling family, dower houses were set aside from the main house to accommodate widows and maiden aunts retired from day-to-day affairs of the family.

Undemocratic by today's standards, the system worked in the 1800s because the immense amount of labor needed to clothe, nourish, shelter and protect the community had to be organized locally. Human and animal muscle power bore the burden of providing the elements of survival and luxuries. But in the 1870s the industrial revolution accelerated the breakdown of the system and foreshadowed closer intermingling of the classes.

It was, in fact, the relentless elimination of the horse and carriage by the railroads and, ultimately, the motor car, that signaled the end of the rural estate as a centralizing force in rural Britain. Professional governing agencies appeared.

But if the great estates became trivialized as focal points of rural life, the political power of the aristocracy continued to rule in Parliament—through compromise and strategic retreat. This long twilight continued until the 1920s.

Meanwhile, grim job prospects fed idleness in the second son. Already bitter that his older brother would inherit all the family's lands he was often drawn into irresponsible lifestyles at London gambling clubs or racetracks. Or perhaps he romanced a married woman, causing instant scandal. These rakes often became the hard-core remittance men—the rotters whose families quite literally ran them off by cutting off their allowance and shifting to an overseas remittance.

Once on the frontier, given time to ponder, even the gentlest exile often regarded his brother as a desperate tenant might view his landlord—a niggardly, penny pincher hogging the benefits for himself. Americans soon grasped England's embarrassment: The words "remittance man" gradually developed sympathetic overtones, especially among American women.

What was true in England was the pattern in Scotland and Ireland as well. The once-pugnacious Scottish nobility long before had surrendered to British public schooling and the pleasures of spending the season in their London townhouses. Across the Irish Sea, patriots sang bitterly:

> Our absentee landlords have left us,
> In London they cut a great dash,
> While their tenants at home in poor Ireland
> Must pay them the rent in hard cash.

But while Ireland never quite capitulated, much of its land was in the hands of powerful Anglo-Irish families loyal to the English crown. These families also suffered from imports as well as from the violence of Irish rebellion. The Beresfords, for example, held their lands by their wits and were accused of being Catholics in Dublin and Protestants in Waterford. One Beresford desperately spent 30,000 pounds to win back his seat after being defeated for Parliament.

But many landed families began to see opportunity in the dilemma of cheap agricultural imports: British capital could finance those cheap imports of grain, wool and meat on the hoof. With interest return under 3 percent in Britain there was every reason to consider investments overseas, where returns often rose to 6 percent.

In the decade following the American Civil War, the Western cattle bonanza burst on the scene. Seemingly overnight, British investors earned millions of pounds and then suffered terrible animal losses in the blizzards of 1886–1887. But while the boom lasted, and even into the next century, it brought thousands of adventuresome Britons to the western plains of the United States and Canada.

Many were serious investors, intent on settlement. Not by coincidence the migration also produced adventurers as well. Families now could send second sons off in good conscience because of the huge cattle profits being made on the plains stretching from Calgary to South Texas. Mining discoveries drew many young men to the Rocky Mountains but not in numbers rivaling ranching, which was the true western bonanza.

The story of the remittance man is not widely known because it is so diffuse. The besotted son of a lord who enlivened the bars of Calgary is familiar to Canadian historians. So is the story of the pathetic Sir Cecil Moon, whose Colorado marriage to a brawling Irishwoman strangely paralleled, decades later, a pioneering radio soap opera, "Our Gal Sunday." Some characters were legends in their own time, but most remittance men lived quietly as recluses or as small ranchers whose existence drew little notice.

The thing they all had in common was that they had family money to help them seek their fortunes. It may have come as a lump settlement; more often it came as a check or money draft— a periodic remittance on a monthly, semiannual or annual schedule. And there were instances when a young man got money by writing home in desperate need. The latter case was frequent when the young gentleman found he was pathetically mismatched against the harsh land he had chosen for settlement.

And they were victimized. Dozens of Britons—not all of them honest—advertised in British publications that for a few hundred pounds they would enroll a young Briton in a ranch school and turn him into a successful cattleman. Often the young man discovered he was merely an unpaid cowboy—confused and inept but unable to go home.

Although much of the story is tragic, remittance men were amusing, too, as in the case of a young man in Alberta who wrote to his father saying that he had purchased a ranch stocked with eight hundred gophers and needed 1,000 pounds to fatten them for market. His English father, not knowing a rodent gopher from a Hereford cow, sent the money.

These articulate English-speaking foreigners were terribly upsetting to Americans. A dirty, unshaven Jacksonian democrat might be illiterate, but he still bristled when a young Englishman addressed him as a servant. He had been taught from childhood that Americans were not servants. He implicitly believed he would rise to wealth through hard work. He resented class in any form.

The American might feel inferior to the articulate, educated Englishman, but among his own kind he was quick to apply the label of remittance man to the young Britons who tried to locate in the West with money from home. Cowboys, particularly, were jealous of the Britisher's paycheck from home.

Many Britons—especially pecuniary, cattlewise Scotsmen—accomplished superb feats in the West and set patterns for farming enterprises that made American agriculture so successful.

But the remittance men were different. They stumbled for lack of training. Some of them really were rascals, and the remittance check was a barrier to keep them overseas. Very few appear to have been a bit slow or suffered from physical defects. But many others, quite innocent but too proud to admit defeat, failed because they felt rejected by a system they couldn't control. The result so often was heavy drinking, gambling and withdrawal.

And for most there was no going home.

✤
_____

How British Pounds Won the West

During the American Revolution, Britain's economy still was agricultural, self-sufficient and managed by landed aristocrats. But the picture changed swiftly with the beginning of the Napoleonic wars and the need to mobilize a huge army. Taxes were raised and imports of raw materials rose rapidly. The great textile mills of Lancashire—dependent on the American South for 80 percent of their cotton—quickly increased production. Banks improved their expertise in handling complex foreign transactions.

When the war ended in 1815, British leaders put a high priority on sustaining the expansion. Plowing up untilled land and putting a pauperized fifth of the population into wartime jobs had been necessary to defeat Napoleon.

But now—with peace at hand—extraordinary measures were needed to maintain industrial output. The government soon realized that the only substitute for military consumption lay in increased foreign trade. So, armed with the weapons of the Industrial Revolution, Britain turned outward.

Banks led their investors to many lands, including the United States. Britain absorbed most of the bonds for building the 7-million-dollar Erie Canal in 1825 and supplied the credit for some 90 million dollars in early U.S. railroads. But this was just a start: Progress fed progress as Americans moved westward to develop lands acquired from France and Spain. British pounds marched in step.

Anxious for better earnings than the 2 to 3 percent paid locally, British investors found rates of 6 to 7 percent widely available abroad. Additionally, as sanitation and health improved, Great Britain's population soared by 10 percent per decade during the mid-nineteenth century. Consumption grew. More than a third of all U.S. exports went to Britain; conversely,

11

nearly half of U.S. imports were British. Even the rough linens worn by American slaves came from British mills. The American Civil War spurred British exports sharply. Jute from India was quickly turned into sandbags for the battlefields. British merchants sold huge quantities of cotton tenting to Confederate and Union buyers alike.

By the 1870s, Britain's investment abroad had reached 1.2 billion pounds, most of it in bonds earning a favorable 6 percent. But a reaction was at hand. The 1846 repeal of Britain's protective Corn Laws allowed rapid growth in foreign food imports. British cattle producers couldn't compete and cheap American beef slowly created a rural backlash. British working-class families—like American buyers of Japanese cars a century later—voted with their pocketbooks to secure the cheaper meat and grain.

Shrewd British investors (including wealthy landowners) seized the opportunity. With financial know-how in place, they correctly surmised that judicious deployment of British pounds in the developing American West would turn the worrisome new cattle industry into a magnificent opportunity. That decision changed the course of Western history.

✣

CHAPTER 2

The First Remittance Man

Waterloo was a totally European battle—the bloody climax of the Napoleonic Wars in 1815. To stand on the high observation hill overlooking this Belgian field of conflict is to open a text on European history: To the left were the French, here were the British and there were the Prussians. So it's a surprise when an American visitor learns that among the tens of thousands locked in that mortal struggle was a young cavalry officer who later would play a major role in the exploration of the American West.

He was Lieutenant William Drummond Stewart, a Scotsman, and he was only nineteen on that day, June 18, 1815, when nearly twenty-five thousand men lost their lives. But this young aristocrat, serving in the fifteenth King's Hussars, led his cavalrymen in charge after charge against the French. When the war was won and the Duke of Wellington's forces were triumphantly disbanded, Stewart was retired on half pay and sent home wearing the Waterloo Medal for exceptional bravery.

Home was Murthly Castle, in Perthshire in eastern Scotland, where his family owned thirty-two thousand acres. His father was Sir George Stewart, seventeenth lord of Grandtully and fifth baronet of Murthly. One might expect a returning hero to find his future assured, with a good family income and land inheritance in prospect.

Not so. Captain Stewart—he was promoted upon discharge—was a second son at a time when primogeniture was the law of the land. John Stewart, born in 1794 and just fourteen months older than William, would get the estate. There was, of course, a 3,000 dollar trust fund set aside for William and similar amounts for three younger brothers—but no property.

William knew the facts of primogeniture. Younger sons were expected to settle for a career in the military or clergy. But William had done the former and the clergy didn't interest him.

He also had a strong temper, so when his father died in 1827 there was instant trouble. William discovered that his brother not only got the estates but was empowered to dole out the small dollops of earnings from William's trust. The two men quarreled so fiercely that, in his final rage, William swore never to sleep another night under the roof of Murthly Castle.

It was his first step in becoming the first prominent remittance man in the American West. He was an impetuous, pleasure-loving explorer of far places who—in serving his own gratifications—did much for American history. And through the workings of fate he finally won it all—the family title and the estates as well. But that was much later.

William's exile after his father's death was self-imposed. The reason, as explained by Western author Marshall Sprague, "His brother, now Sir John, sixth baronet of Murthly, gave him just enough money to encourage him to stay away from the castle." That is exactly how the American frontier defined a remittance man—a younger son paid to live abroad.

His exile didn't happen all at once. William hunted and explored Europe until, during a visit home, romance blossomed.

Even his love affairs bore Stewart's special cachet. Two authors, Mae Reed Porter and Odessa Davenport, in their 1963 book *Scotsman in Buckskin*, gave the following account:

> It probably was sometime in 1829 that Captain Stewart visited a nearby farm house belonging to his friends, the Atholls, who were connections of Lord Glenlyon. Here in the courtyard he saw an extraordinarily beautiful girl, her skirts tucked up until they barely covered her knees, and immediately William lost his head, if not his heart. A contemporary said, "He fell in love with her nether limbs

when he saw her tromping blankets in a tub." The girl's name was Christina Stewart—no relation to the Stewart family—and she was working on the Atholl farm as a maid. Legends are still told by the villagers of Dunkeld concerning the beauty of her face and character. That the handsome Captain Stewart roused in Christina a full measure of love and devotion no one who reads her story can doubt.

Christina bore Captain Stewart's son. The child was named George, after William's father. A few months later Captain

Christina Stewart, a beautiful Scottish servant, bore Stewart a son out of wedlock. In an act unusual for an aristocrat, Stewart married her and legitimized his heir. But the son, after winning the Victoria Cross in Crimea, died mysteriously in a duel or a drunken fall. (Courtesy Hastings House.)

Stewart and Christina were married in Edinburgh. Little George was brought to the ceremony for purposes of legitimization, as provided by Scottish law. (Years later when William financed a family history, George's birthday was advanced so he would appear to have been born after the marriage.)

But there was to be no family life for William. He lodged Christina and George in an Edinburgh apartment and began planning an exotic hunting trip—in the far west of North America.

His marriage to Christina, a girl of inferior social standing, had raised questions about his stability (most aristocratic sons merely had their fun and didn't marry the girl), and now rumor spread about his foolhardy plans to live among savage Indians. No doubt some members of the family were glad to see him go.

His ship docked in New York in May 1832. Slowly working his way west, he arrived in the bustling riverfront town of St. Louis, a major jumping-off place for the West. His distinguished family name soon put him in touch with William Sublette, a fur trade pioneer affiliated with the Rocky Mountain Fur Company. Sublette introduced Stewart to his partner, Robert Campbell. The following spring when Campbell assembled a large pack train to carry trade goods and liquor to the 1833 summer rendezvous in the Green River country (in what today is Wyoming), Stewart joined up. His latest remittance from Scotland just covered the 500 dollar fee Campbell asked of his neophyte mountain man. The party left St. Louis on April 13, 1833.

The concourse of forty men and several hundred animals (including sheep to be eaten until the traders reached buffalo country) followed the Missouri River, then branched northwest to the Platte River—a route soon to be called the Oregon Trail— and crossed South Pass on July 2. Reaching the juncture of the Green River and Horse Creek, the present site of a Wyoming town called Daniel, the Rocky Mountain Fur Company was ready for business.

The rendezvous were great trade fairs and the trappers, mountain men and Indians dressed their best and outfitted their women for the occasion. Stewart donned a white leather hunting jacket and multihued Stewart clan plaid trousers, cutting as colorful a figure as any of the painted, feather-bedecked Indians from the villages camped nearby. No one laughed; the veteran of Waterloo was an excellent rifleman and horseman.

But, as summed up by Porter and Davenport, the fur trade was serious enterprise:

> This was big business in which Robert Campbell and William Sublette were engaged—how big, it is difficult to realize now. Every man of any consequence, actual or imagined, in the states, in England, and on the continent of Europe owned at least one beaver hat. China's appetite for furs was insatiable since their wealthy people preferred to wear their heating arrangements rather than install them in their homes. Captain Stewart was [in the midst] of the largest, wildest rendezvous ever held in the Rocky Mountains—or anywhere else.

But the Indians from the many assembled tribes caught Stewart's fancy, and he wrote two autobiographical books centering on this romantic fascination. His prose was heavily larded with romantic nonsense about male homosexuals in the tribes who, like the eunuchs of old, kept the squaws in line.

Harking back to his affair with Christina, it's scarcely surprising that Stewart bedded at least two Indian maidens. In one of his books he described Tona, a fifteen-year-old Crow, as "a wild creature, scantily clothed, with well-formed limbs, beautiful hands and arms, and a roguish eye, half-concealed by long lashes."

Nether limbs again, one supposes. Describing his meeting with another girl, Stewart claims that "her eyes opened with almost supernatural light and gleamed on me with wild excitement."

Stewart met legendary frontiersman Captain Bonneville, mountain man Jim Bridger and Tom Fitzpatrick. The latter, as fieldman for the Rocky Mountain Fur Company, had hired a hunter, Antoine Clement, a half-breed who became Stewart's life-long friend and even spent time in Murthly Castle.

After the rendezvous ended in late July, Stewart joined a trapping trip headed eastward to the Big Horn Mountains. The record of what he did next isn't clear. Possibly he and Jim Bridger went south to Taos to explore the manifold charms of New Spain. No mention of nether limbs but knowing the captain's roving eye one wonders.

Stewart kept returning to the annual rendezvous for most of the decade. He saw the fur industry rise and fall, with the assemblages growing ever smaller (although the magnitude of the drinking and revelry seemed to remain constant).

He wintered on the West Coast after the 1835 rendezvous, mostly at Fort Vancouver (Portland, Oregon). It was here that he met Dr. John McLoughlin, the Hudson's Bay Company's Columbia Basin representative. McLoughlin was a huge Canadian of Scots ancestry and lived in a baronial castle that doubtless made Stewart feel at home. Stewart sympathized with Dr. McLoughlin's mission of colonizing the region for Britain—amidst growing friction with Americans—but his main concern seems to have been the impact of all settlement on the magnificent West.

Stewart hadn't lost this concern when he met the Presbyterian missionaries, Dr. Marcus and Narcissa Whitman, on a later trip—his 1836 rendezvous journey with Tom Fitzpatrick. After meeting in what today is Nebraska, the two parties sat together on the prairie for afternoon tea near the Platte River.

After eating some of Narcissa's fresh-baked bread, Stewart is reported to have said, "I have been West before, and want to come again before civilization closes in. Now that ladies are making the overland journey, I perceive the beginning of the end of this wild domain."

Narcissa, the first white woman to cross the Rocky Mountains to Oregon, then asked, "Shall you be sorry to see it pass?"

"Frankly, Mrs. Whitman, yes." Stewart then quoted a verse from the poet, William Cullen Bryant:

> ... these
> The unshorn fields, boundless and beautiful,
> For which the speech of England has no name—
> The Prairies ...

Stewart thus appears to have been an early environmentalist. He made the most of the western experience while it lasted.

For nearly seven years after his first trip in 1832 he joined the long caravans beyond the Missouri. He paid shipping costs to send two live buffalo and a live grizzly bear to Scotland, where his friend, Lord Breadalbane, displayed them to the public. Even Queen Victoria, on a visit to Balmoral, noted in her diary that she saw Lord Breadalbane's American buffaloes.

Stewart's life now took a fateful turn that facilitated his greatest achievement—the commissioning of Alfred Jacob Miller to make historic paintings of the West. In late 1836 William had written to his brother demanding release of the 3,000-pound trust fund. Sir John's reply, which William received in New Orleans in early 1837, was probably a model for all the hundreds of letters that British heads of families were to send to their remittance men for the next sixty or seventy years. Sir John said— after pointing out that Murthly Castle was being enlarged at heavy cost—that he couldn't send the trust funds. Sorry.

If William went into a rage at the response, he soon quieted down because of another letter—this one apparently from his wife, Christina. She informed him that Sir John was dying of cancer and would be without a direct heir.

One can imagine the gloating in New Orleans, where William had business interests (including cotton investments). He would soon be Sir William Drummond Stewart. He would possess the estates. Because he had married Christina in a public ceremony, young George would be his lawful heir. But for the moment he needed large oil paintings of his western adventures to decorate the walls of Murthly Castle when he went home to claim his estate.

He wanted constant reminders of the West—the Indians and trappers, the great peaks and valleys of his beloved American wilderness.

New Orleans friends told Stewart about Miller, twenty-six, who had recently opened a portrait studio at 132 Chartres Street. A native of Baltimore, Miller had shown enough talent to earn from his family the money for art studies in France and Italy, including a tour of the Alps. Home again in 1834, Miller had little success as a painter. But when he moved to New Orleans in 1836 his portraiture attracted favorable comment.

Still, when Stewart entered his studio in April 1837, and proposed that Miller join a safari to the Indian country, the young artist (after checking Stewart's credentials with the British consul) speedily agreed.

Miller was enchanted with the West. His enthusiastic water-color sketches (many of which later were transferred to oils) produced the romantic themes Stewart had in mind. Indian warriors, historic Fort Laramie, the animals and mountain landscapes of the West all went into Miller's sketchbook. He was painting from sheer joy. "He did not know that he was the first man in all time to fully paint the actual Rockies," wrote the 1963 biographers.

Nor could Miller know that within a few decades many of the things he painted—the Indian way of life, the wild mountain men and the great herds of buffalo—would be gone forever.

He and Stewart had early difficulties. Stewart was an inflexible disciplinarian and insisted that Miller take guard duty at night like everyone else. Miller thus was too tired to paint Stewart's pictures. Stewart relented only to this extent: He would allow the painter to hire a replacement for guard duty.

Stewart possessed a huge London-made rifle which fired a ball nearly an inch in diameter. The projectile was so slow, however, that it wasn't much good for killing. But Miller and Antoine Clement found that the heavy ball—fired at a buffalo's skull—would stun the beast just long enough to give Miller time for a quick sketch before the animal recovered and ran off.

Stewart's party returned by way of Fort Laramie, arriving in St. Louis in October. Miller was sent south to New Orleans with orders to begin making oil paintings from his watercolor sketches. He worked through the winter and summer of 1838. He did not accompany Stewart's 1838 foray into the fur country.

Miller draws criticism today for his romantic style, but he pleased his patron. When word of his paintings spread, a New York gallery invited Miller to do a public showing. This was in 1839 when Stewart was embarking for Scotland to claim his titles and, among other things, hang Miller's paintings. His brother had died in 1838.

Stewart didn't seem to be in a hurry to go home, but under his saturnine exterior he must have been full of anticipation.

When Miller asked permission to extract and show eighteen of his Western paintings from the shipments bound for Scotland, Stewart gave quick approval. The showing drew immense critical and public acclaim and resulted in an extension of the display period. At twenty-nine, Miller was famous, and Stewart asked him to come to Scotland the following year to paint even larger pictures of the West.

Miller not only painted but maintained a firm friendship with his patron, even to the point of serving as host at castle social functions when the frenetic Sir William was off on a jaunt. Miller finally returned to the United States, where he and Stewart had a brief reunion in 1842 in Baltimore. (Sir William had returned for a last tour of his beloved West.)

Back in Scotland for good in 1844, Sir William caused one ruckus after another, engaging in petty fights with his relatives and suing in court to overturn the law of entail that enforced the rule of primogeniture. Why Stewart wanted to destroy the law that had belatedly delivered him the estate isn't clear. He ultimately withdrew the suit.

And he made good on his pledge never to sleep beneath Murthly's roof. He had a bedroom built high on the castle wall, much like a swallow's nest, that was connected by doorway to the interior. The irony of having to sleep outside a castle he owned was lost in the welter of Stewart's stubbornness.

Perhaps his days as a remittance man had twisted him. Or perhaps he never talked about the searing images his mind still held fresh from Waterloo. He had tremendous strengths and weaknesses. Liquor and a terrible temper were among the latter. According to one story, a Murthly laboring man was asked if he had ever seen Sir William the worse for liquor. He replied, "No, my lord—but I have many times seen him the better for it."

He rejected domestic life but he couldn't get along without female alliances. He and Christina—called Lady Stewart after William's knighthood—kept in touch. Their son, George, received a good education and an army commission through family influence. As a lieutenant in the Light Brigade of the ninety-third Highlanders, serving in the Crimean War, he led the famous charge immortalized by Alfred, Lord Tennyson, and was one of the fortunate survivors of that futile attack on November 25, 1854. Like his father, he came home a hero.

Sir William and Lady Christina were together the next year in London to watch as their son was awarded the Victoria Cross for heroism. It was an occasion that might have presaged family unity, with George ultimately succeeding his father at Murthly.

Nothing like that happened. Christina died of tuberculosis soon after the ceremony in London. In 1868, Major George Stewart died mysteriously, either in a duel or from falling down a stairway while intoxicated. Sir William died in 1871 at seventy-five, bitterly fighting legal wars to the end. As a convert to Roman Catholicism, he feared that his heir apparent, younger brother Archibald, who was a Protestant and a Mason, would strip the estate's chapel of its religious artwork, which William had commissioned. Those fears were realized when Archibald became twentieth lord of Grandtully and eighth baronet of Murthly.

Sir William soon faded from memory. Hundreds of his letters, including many to and from America, lay uncataloged in an Edinburgh lawyer's vault—an historical treasure trove not discovered until the 1950s. Meanwhile, it took Americans many years to realize just how priceless the Miller paintings were in terms of recording the West as it had been.

Sir William's old age might have been happier if he could have shared his wife's perspective. When she was dying Christina was asked if she would make a will. She replied, "No. I brought nothing to the estate and I will take nothing from it."

By contrast Stewart wanted it all, possibly a reflection of his bitterness in the role of a once-landless remittance man. He now wanted to tighten his grip, even from the grave.

To this end he adopted the son of one of his long-time Texas friends in 1869 to try to avoid Archibald's succession. Franc Nichols, the young Texan, embraced the idea, but the courts soon rejected Stewart's ploy. Even so, Franc looted Murthly of many valuables. He sold many of Miller's paintings at auctions in Edinburgh at distress prices. Many other Stewart treasures were shipped to Texas, where they became part of Franc's estate and were inherited by his descendants.

Sir William's efforts thus boomeranged. The land he tried so desperately to keep was lost in bitter struggle. And the artwork and written records of his adventures—which today are so valuable—were sacrificed in his frantic effort to keep the land from his brother, Archibald. The things that could have become his monument were scattered like aspen leaves on a Wyoming mountainside in late autumn.

❖
_____

A Man in the Shadows

Falling between two worlds, the legendary remittance man holds a powerful and mysterious grip on writers. One of the century's most successful, James Michener, used the theme in 1946 when he wrote his war novel *Tales of the South Pacific*. One chapter centers on a remittance man, an unseen Englishman in the Solomon Islands. Michener's shabby hero spies on Japanese forces and sends vital shortwave messages on enemy deployment to the Allies fighting inch by bloody inch for Guadalcanal.

In the end, of course, the Japanese run him to ground but not before his broadcasts help U.S. forces inflict heavy damage as the enemy is driven from the Solomons. Grateful young American officers, charmed by his cheerful radio greeting—beginning with, "This is your remittance man speaking"—are curious about his identity. They discover that he is an outcast from Britain—a planter named Anderson who married a black island woman. His personal life, however, remains a mystery.

When his island is captured, the Americans find the destroyed native village which harbored him. They discover that the Japanese have left behind a long line of picket posts, each surmounted by a skull. They identify one skull as that of the Englishman, with a stream of army ants, in Michener's words, "giving the remittance man their ancient jungle burial." He has risen above the rejections of his own kind.

Failure, redemption and death—these are the mileposts of the remittance man. But are they truth? Or merely the desire of later-day readers to have the British second son perform on a stage we have created for him? And must there always be disgrace?

In literature, yes. Early in the century, Hamlin Garland, Pulitzer Prize winner in 1921, used the same theme in a short fiction story about a callow English lad named Lester. Lester is

24

studying to be a cattle rancher in Colorado. However, when his family's 50-dollar-a-month remittances expire, Lester—spineless and inept—hasn't the courage to strike out on his own. He meekly accepts a joyless marriage arranged with the rancher's illiterate daughter.

But even in real life, the stories passed down through the decades deal bluntly with the remittance man. In northern Wyoming there is a recurrent story of a Briton killed in a fall from a cliff. His body was kept frozen all winter until the spring thaw permitted burial. A historical marker, noting his death and referring to him as a remittance man, marks the site.

So a remittance man is usually a victim. Whether in the American West or elsewhere, he evokes sympathy as the castaway of an outmoded social system. In Canada he often dies of a broken heart. In Australia, too, he cannot cope. The Australian national ballad, "Waltzing Matilda," is about a swagman (very likely a remittance man) who drowns himself in a billabong rather than face arrest for stealing a sheep. He is acting out the alienation felt by thousands of migrating Englishmen against the aristocratic excesses of England.

✤

CHAPTER 3

An Era Gone,
the Land Remains

Britain's heritage of great estates has foundations rooted in suffering and blood, in courage and strength. They were created by a system—primogeniture—that remained virtually indestructible for eight hundred years. But when the system collapsed in the twentieth century, what was left was a hollow shell, its past glories now mostly for show—but what a show it still remains.

The Ridge in Gloucestershire is a good example of the collapse, even though it was not a grand estate ruled by a duke or marquis. Its families were not aristocrats but landed gentry and only locally distinguished, although Piers Bengough, a descendant, today is Queen Elizabeth's representative at Ascot. Its origins are lost in time; its written history dates back only two hundred years.

And yet one member of the family, Emily M. Bengough (pronounced Ben-goff), who was born at The Ridge and grew up there, left a poignant account of life in the great halls of the mansion, in the well-staffed workrooms and in the woods and fields that produced the estate's income. The beige stones of the mansion are gone, along with the two huge couchant lions flanking the front entrance, but Emily's story of the 1880s lives on.

Life there was very beautiful, especially if you were a small child, as Emily was in the 1870s. And it must have been a difficult place to leave, whether you were Emily or her older brother, Clement, who became a remittance man living in a rough-hewn, sod-roofed cabin in a dry Wyoming valley.

What made family life on an estate so pleasant, beside the beauties and pleasures of nature, was privilege. Tenant farmers did the field labor while servants made life inside the mansion comfortable, civilized and genteel. Being a landlord, either aristocratic or landed gentry, was a most desirable state of affairs. Whether you were a duke or a humble squire you were part of the nation's power elite.

Even when that power had become symbolic, it still was lordly and impressive. Emily remembered riding in a wonderful carriage reserved ceremonially for her father, John Charles Bengough, when he was high sheriff of Gloucestershire in 1877. There were coachmen atop the carriage, footmen at the rear and the high sheriff's coat-of-arms richly embossed on the sides. In other parts of Britain children barely older than Emily were already working in the coal mines.

The Bengoughs were part of a new urban class of landlords. This class of gentry steadily gained power and influence in the early 1900s. The growing economic power of urban commerce—industrialism, manufacture and trade with the colonies—created sources of wealth independent of the land. These families of the new class also wanted to live in great manor houses in the country—and they had the money.

Some estates, of course, were locked up under the ancient system of entail, originally intended to ensure loyalty to the crown. They couldn't be sold except by act of Parliament. But there were other lands that could be purchased directly as single estates, or individual smallholdings could be combined under one ownership.

The latter was the case at The Ridge near the Gloucestershire town of Wotton-Under-Edge. A strange name with a simple origin: In medieval times it was referred to as the "wool town under the edge" of the Cotswold escarpment, thus "Wotton-Under-Edge." As the name implies, the area had many sheep. The Cotswold Hills are notable for their magnificent scenic views. And the estate called The Ridge has an outstanding one—an outlook down into the Severn Valley eight hundred feet below and across to the Welsh Hills in the far distance. So no wonder a squire had built a manor house there in the eighteenth century.

And no wonder, either, that early in the nineteenth century a cloth merchant, Edward Sheppard, was attracted to The Ridge. With his bank account bulging from selling uniforms to the British Army during the Napoleonic Wars, Sheppard decided that he, too, would become a country squire. He razed the former house on the site and commissioned a famous landscape architect, Humphrey Repton, to design an estate with a three-story mansion as centerpiece. It was an imposing work. Three large rooms were spread across the west-facing Severn overlook—a drawing room, a library and a dining room. They were given connecting doors so they could be opened into one splendid hall. There were twenty-eight bedrooms.

It was finished in 1825 and, soon thereafter, so was Edward Sheppard. The death of Napoleon on St. Helena in 1821 symbolized the period of peace that had settled on Europe. The market for military uniforms dropped precipitously and so did Sheppard's bank account. His creditors put him up for liquidation in 1837.

At midcentury the Bengough family from nearby Bristol purchased his estate. Emily's grandfather, George, was the first of the Bengough owners and, when he died in 1856, his first son, George, moved into The Ridge. But he died in 1865 and, having had only daughters, the law of primogeniture put his next eldest brother, John Charles, into The Ridge.

The Bengoughs were bankers, and being a Bristol banker in those days—before the banks were consolidated—meant great profit, especially in a city with a strong sea trade with the New World. Bristol bankers, in fact, financed much of the slave trade to the Caribbean and the southern United States.

Emily Bengough was born at The Ridge on October 23, 1869, one of twin daughters. Even as a child she was impressed by the view beyond the terrace and tennis courts and decades later wrote of "the glorious woods beyond the park, the vale below them, the silver Severn and the soft blue, distant Welsh and Malvern Hills."

The Ridge was actually a small village (it took a staff of fifty to run the place) so Emily's childhood was a near-continuous round of adventure. After morning Bible reading, she and her sister and a younger brother (there were seven older children as well) played in the woods, sniffed flowers in the conservatory, talked with the servants or watched the blacksmith make sparks fly at the forge. As children of the landlord they were honored visitors when they cadged sweets in the cottages of the older, semiretired servants.

Tenants gathered annually in the landlord's justice room where they paid their rents, made contracts and discussed other matters concerning farming the estate's thousands of acres. Emily also remembered social events to which the wives of the tenants were invited. Servants—groomsmen, stable hands, chambermaids, a teacher for the staff children, a pastor for the small church on the site, plus laundresses, personal servants and kitchen staff—were salaried. Emily and her siblings did not attend regular school but were tutored by a German woman, Fraulein Emmerlich, who lived at The Ridge.

As Emily wrote in her narrative of the 1880s, the Bengoughs were a happy family. The boys and even the girls were aggressive cricket players and had an active social life. They sang frequently as a family choir, hiring an organist from nearby Wotton-Under-Edge to play as an accompanist. John Bengough and his older sons, including Clement, joined in enthusiastically.

Noblesse oblige functioned to bring the family and servants together on holidays. Emily also recalled that, when a gardener's small niece died, the Bengoughs arranged a service at which family members gathered at the drawing-room piano to sing, "Tender Shepherd, Thou has stilled now Thy little lamb's brief weeping."

Fox hunts were great fun because the children could romp with the large pack of hounds assembled for the chase. Guy Fawkes day was a special event at which the Bengough's tower of sticks, when lighted, made a bonfire visible across the Severn. They roasted potatoes afterward in the embers.

But estate profits were dropping under the impact of imported grain and meat from abroad, and in 1895 the family moved to the Ridings, a dower house, to save money. A dower house was maintained on many estates for the widow when her eldest son and daughter-in-law took charge of the mansion. But in this case the entire family moved and rented The Ridge to a Colonel Parkinson. The colonel and his son both were killed in World War I.

Emily's reminiscences were selective. Being several years younger than her older brothers, she seldom referred to them, except to describe them as six feet tall and very good cricket players. John Alan, the eldest, and Clement were captains of cricket teams at their public schools, Marlborough and Rugby respectively.

She skipped over the bad news, telling nothing of the family heartache and the prospect of impoverishment that must have led to Clement's decision to seek his fortune in Wyoming. He was painfully shy and, as he grew older, he shunned family social functions. Did he also have an unhappy love affair? Or did he, like other remittance men, simply feel family pressure to get out of the way so his brother, John Alan, could have a free hand to run the estate when their father died?

The Ridge, luxurious mansion in Gloucestershire of the Bengough family. It was from here that young Clement Bengough departed for Wyoming and a cattleman's life. The mansion was razed in 1934. (Photo courtesy of the American Heritage Center, University of Wyoming.)

Nor did Emily discuss the deaths of John Alan, in 1899, and of her father in 1913. These deaths, plus the tragic and untimely death of Emily's nephew, John Alan's eldest son, John Crosbie Bengough, on a World War I battlefield in 1916, contributed to the loss of the Bengough estate. Family leadership faltered and the decision was taken to sell The Ridge. But the family still managed to finance the construction of a beautiful and moving stone monument in John Crosbie's memory on a road near The Ridge.

The Ridge briefly became an army convalescent home operated for returning soldiers, but in 1919 it was transformed into a hotel—a desperate gamble many landed families attempted in the disastrous economic climate of the post-World War I era. But, like the cloth merchant before them, the Bengough's cycle had run its course. In 1919, a new ownership emerged, demonstrating how property ebbs and flows with national economic trends.

Emily Bengough closes her *Memories of My Victorian Childhood* with a short poem about the darkening of the sky at sunset over the Severn River, a prophetic vision of the Bengough's last look from the beautiful windows of The Ridge.

Perhaps Clement Bengough, who arrived in Wyoming in 1886 or 1887, was spared much of his sister's sadness by leaving The Ridge before the worst times set in and while he was still in his mid-twenties. He went back to England for a visit many years later, but there is no record of whom he saw or what he thought about his family's drift away from The Ridge. One can only speculate on his reaction at seeing the great mansion slowly falling into ruin, much as his own youthful dreams of ranching success.

As a boy at The Ridge he must have read a good deal about the glamorous American West—its cowboys and vast herds of cattle. He must have developed romantic notions as well, an insight visualized by American historian Robert G. Athearn, who said of British expectations, "An American cattle ranch might even offer something more than just a place to make money. To many an Englishman who liked to ride and to hunt there was promise of a feudal-type domain in the Far West where the herdsman cared for his property while he and his companions rode after antelope."

Clement began his Wyoming career with high hopes. After working in 1887 for the Gresley-Robbins Ranch near Laramie to learn ranching—with his family paying a remittance to the rancher to teach their son to be independent—he struck out on his own. But the remittances had to keep coming because the son was having trouble achieving independence.

It was a hard, bitter life he had contracted for. At twenty-six, he was physically strong and well educated in Latin and good literature. But that didn't ensure success as a cattle rancher. Ranch schooling might help some but it didn't provide capital. Clement gradually realized his family would never be able to give him much more than a small stake. He became a lonesome misfit by the time he took over a homestead near the mining camp of Morgan, at the base of Wyoming's Snowy Range, thirty miles northwest of Laramie.

Gradually, he became an experienced rancher, but he remained his own herdsman. He was proud of his British-bred Herefords and he made small amounts of money from the sale of steers. But he continued to welcome the small remittances from England. He had good horses and perhaps took better care of them than he did of himself.

His living quarters were primitive. His cabin, with a dirt floor as well as a sod roof, had a cooking stove which served also for warmth. The cabin's one door opened to a view of the knife-sharp clarity of the Wyoming skyline—just as beautiful in its contrast as the soft, misty view from The Ridge. Irene McCormick, a young girl who lived at nearby Morgan, recalled a visit to Bengough's place when she was ten or eleven, about 1912. She had heard that Bengough was a British remittance man—but didn't know what the phrase meant.

Her impromptu stop resulted from a sudden snowstorm. She was a passenger on the stage from Laramie, a horse-drawn covered wagon, and the storm was so severe the driver drove to Bengough's cabin for refuge from the blinding snow. Irene and other passengers stayed for two hours with Bengough before the driver felt safe in resuming the journey.

Years later the cabin had degenerated to a pile of rotting logs and boards. But earlier, as Irene McCormick remembered:

> It was a single room, rectangular, with a dirt floor. Bengough was there, being very nice, and there were lots of books. He was nice looking with very blue eyes. He was about six feet tall and dressed in casual attire: khaki pants and English boots that were pretty well beat up. And for outdoor work he always wore a flat cap, not a Stetson.

Then she added, "But the thing I'll never forget is the stench. He hunted animals for profit, mostly coyotes, and he stretched the skins flesh side out over boards to dry. And these were stored at one end of the room and the smell was terrible."

People liked Bengough, but he soon got a reputation as an eccentric, a man of strange likes and dislikes. He had a favorite mare called Martha, that could jump fences and save him the trouble of opening gates. But local storytellers say that Martha refused to jump a fence one day and Bengough killed her with a pistol shot between the ears. Yet he loved animals in his own rough, sporting way. To hunt wolves and coyotes he kept a pack of Siberian wolfhounds—huge beasts so ferocious Bengough reportedly carried a club when he entered their cage to feed them.

On one occasion cowboys in the Morgan area treed a bear and pulled it down with a rope. Bengough asked them not to kill it because (he told them mischievously) he had always wanted to wrestle a bear. The contest took place, with the bear savaging Bengough so severely the cowboys soon pulled him away for first-aid treatment.

If Bengough ever regretted his Wyoming life he never complained. As a joke he once paid a bill from his Laramie bank account by making the check out in Latin. His banker chuckled and cashed the check.

And he loved gambling. He once bet neighboring cowboys a dozen Stetson hats and a jug of whiskey that he had a steer that weighed a ton. The cowboys took the bet, allowing ninety pounds of shrinkage when Bengough drove his bovine heavyweight to a railroad siding for shipment. The animal weighed in at 1,910 pounds and Bengough won his bet.

He was gruff, but he often came to Morgan to chat with Irene McCormick and her grandmother, with whom Irene lived. He found Irene a good listener when he talked of his literary interests. His friends were few. Yet his neighbors respected him, and when he died at seventy-three, they buried him on a lonely hillside near his cabin. A large granite shaft surrounded by iron palings bears this inscription, including a verse from Robert Louis Stevenson:

> Clement S. Bengough
> 19 Nov. 1934
> This is the verse you grave for me
> Here he lies where he longed to be;
> Home is the sailor, home from sea
> And the hunter home from the hill.

Meanwhile, The Ridge back at Wotton-Under-Edge was under new management. A new cycle was beginning and, again, it was war and its aftermath that played a major part.

As Edward Sheppard, the nineteenth-century cloth merchant, had occupied the stage at Wotton-Under-Edge and then disappeared, a second cycle now had dispensed with the Bengoughs. Economics had put small bankers like the Bengoughs at the mercy of national branch banking—and war finished them off. So The Ridge now fell to the Cory family, shipping and coal magnates from Cardiff, Wales.

The family of John Cory, a Welsh ship owner, had lost twenty ships to German U-boats in World War I. With his insurance money from the ship sinkings John Cory bought The Ridge and the five hundred acres that remained in 1919. At that time the earl of Berkeley was trying to raise money to repair Berkeley Castle, so the Corys bought part of his ten thousand acres to add to their holdings at The Ridge.

After inheritance laws changed in the 1920s it was no longer a simple matter for owners like the Corys to leave the estates to the eldest sons. But a caring, concerned family could still find ways to hang onto property and use it cooperatively for benefit of the whole family. The Corys did this. The present owner is Raymond Cory, grandson of John, who died in 1931. Having taken over the estate from his father in 1962, he is The Ridge's third generation of Corys. He grew up in the Vale of Glamorgan outside Cardiff, but he remembers The Ridge when he visited as a boy:

> Grandfather used to have shooting parties up here. The house was not in a good state of repair—and unfurnished—but he used to get the gamekeepers' wives to put up trestle tables and provide lunch for the shooting parties. I was born in 1922 so I was 9 when my grandfather died. ...
>
> Then my father had it and the place was almost impossible to deal with. It had twenty-eight bedrooms and one bathroom. It was built on a grand scale.

The paucity of bathrooms? Cory easily explains, "When you wanted a bath in those times a servant brought a tub and hot water to your room and you bathed in front of the fireplace." A quaint fact, not unlike learning that Winston Churchill, that marvelous symbol of British aristocracy, never in his long lifetime ever dressed himself.

Raymond Cory agrees with Emily Bengough about the view from the manor house. He loves the site. Although the great mansion is gone, he recalls that it was made of Bath stone, which is a soft beige color. It faced west and had one of the finest views in Gloucestershire—eight hundred feet above sea level and five and one-half miles as the crow flies from the Severn.

But saving the estate was, in the opinion of an architect, possible only if a family could afford to live there and spend thousands of pounds to keep it up. So reluctantly The Ridge was battered into the ground in the mid-1930s. It died hard. There are old men in Wotton-Under-Edge who remember playing as boys in its collapsed hallways and looting it for souvenirs. But Raymond Cory's father exercised one piece of excellent judgment. He took his architect's advice to save the stable courtyard.

Made of the beautiful buff Cotswold stone mined from local quarries, the stable courtyard includes in its U-shape the kitchen quarters once attached to the big house, along with the servant's quarters in the other arm of the "U." The tall central doorways of the coach house, where horse-drawn carriages entered, have been turned into immense picture windows, behind which is a spacious living room.

The kitchen is still a kitchen. But the Corys have turned the servants' quarters into apartments for themselves and their three daughters, whose families live there or use it on recreation trips from London or Cardiff. Framed at the end of a large driveway, the home is impressively large to American eyes. A stable? It looks more like a mansion along the Hudson River.

Raymond Cory looks at the future:

> I have 400 of the original 500 acres, of which 250 are farmland and 150 are woodland. I have one tenant today. He lives in the house at Bowcote Farm [the name of The Ridge's agricultural enterprise.] The estate is mostly dairy, a mixed farm, milking forty cows with some beef stock, sheep and pigs and grows some cereals. The tenant pays me a rent.

> The farm tenant survives because his wife, his mother and his brother work. They employ one man and they can make a living out of it. But if they had to employ a lot of labor, with the rates that farm workers get nowadays—10,000 pounds a year—they just couldn't make it pay.

And Cory has worked hard to keep the land in the family: "To give away land to heirs requires seven years' notice [to the government]. After four years the tax rate comes down from 40 percent to 30 percent, then to 10 percent and then to nil at seven years."

His wife, Betty, pilots Phoebe, a Massey tractor. It takes two hours to cut a huge expanse of lawn. The old tractor, which cost 250 pounds in 1950, burns low-cost fuel oil but will pull a two-bottom plow. However, no expansion of farming is in prospect. The government is encouraging farmers to turn land into timber and golf courses.

Raymond Cory has met Piers Bengough, nephew of young John Crosbie Bengough, who died in World War I, and the two have reminisced about the old days of primogeniture that drove so many younger sons overseas even though they were unprepared for hard work to establish themselves. They were a breed apart, Cory explains:

You go back in time to the Norman Conquest. The families were given these lands in return for supporting William the Conqueror. Families didn't work. They administered the big estates but as to actually working at a profession, they didn't. They were landed gentry with big families who didn't work with their hands.

He whimsically recites this ditty:

> Lord Lucas went to mend the light.
> It shocked him dead and served him right,
> It is the duty of the gentleman,
> Always to employ the artisan.

One suspects Clement Bengough's ghost would understand his dictum, even in the lonely hills of far-off Wyoming. It explains why, through centuries of British culture, land ownership became tied inextricably to the concept of being a gentleman. Fate dealt Clement Bengough an impossible hand but he, with his jumping horses and coursing hounds, remained a perfect British gentleman on the rocky prairies of Wyoming, just a bit down on his luck.

Adjoining the Cory's vacation home is the lawn-covered enclosure nearly fifty yards long where The Ridge once stood. In its way it is sacred ground, and on a moonlight night it wouldn't take much imagination to see strange shapes returned from afar and from times past speak to each other about a world now gone forever. You might even hear Clement Bengough galloping through the woods with his savage wolfhounds.

❖
_____

American Remittance Men?

Were there American remittance men? Not in the narrow sense, because inheritance laws in the United States permitted sons and daughters to share equally in the family estate (unless altered by a will). Thus, the younger sons who wandered the globe as disinherited black sheep tended to be British, not American.

But that doesn't mean there weren't scores of young Ivy League gentlemen bounding up and down the Rocky Mountains and across the plains late in the nineteenth century. Teddy Roosevelt, a Harvard man, ranched in the Dakotas and hunted big game in Colorado. The distinguished Penrose family of Philadelphia, despairing of their youngest son, Spencer, allowed him to leave Harvard to seek his fortune in Cripple Creek—which he soon acquired. Sinking his golden grubstake from Colorado into an even richer prospect in Utah's great Bingham copper pit, enabled Penrose to purchase the luxurious Broadmoor Hotel in Colorado Springs and give millions to charity. Another Harvard man, Owen Wister, came to Wyoming to adventure and wrote that all-time classic Western, *The Virginian*.

Edmund (Ned) Randolph, whose family helped found Princeton University, dropped out of that institution to become an adventurer in the West early in the twentieth century. He rebelled against what he called the stereotyped life of New York and worked as a Montana cowboy long enough to learn ranching. He became a wealthy cattleman and author of Western lore.

Another Princetonian was Horace Devereaux, who raised 100,000 dollars from British investors to build the splendid Hotel Colorado in the west slope spa of Glenwood Springs. He also organized one of the West's earliest polo clubs, almost on the heels of the departing ponies of the Ute Indians.

And still they come. A restaurant owner in Aspen once touched on the expatriate phenomenon in resort communities by explaining (with tongue only partly in cheek) how he managed his personnel: "When a waitress tells you what hours she wants to work, you are inclined to listen seriously. She just may have enough telephone company stock back in her room to buy you out."

The mountain-ringed Wyoming community of Sheridan, featuring a mild climate because its altitude is only thirty-seven hundred feet, draws many wealthy people—some quite young—living on "old" money. But Milton Chilcott, long-time newspaperman at Sheridan, says the modern remittance man or woman is unobtrusive and not easy to identify:

> They live quietly and they come from everywhere so they aren't identifiable as a class anymore. The British came first, of course, and the first dude ranches were started here when the railroad came. But the Americans have kept up the tradition. You still can adventure in the mountains or play a bit of polo at the Big Horn Club. It is one of the oldest in the United States.

Few will mourn the disappearance of the American aristocrats. To frontier folk they were almost as baffling as the class-conscious British. A good example of the cultural abrasiveness comes from the Black Hills of South Dakota, where a group of wealthy, educated Britons and Americans joined in the 1880s to form a cattle ranching venture headed by Harry Oelrichs, a Baltimore entrepreneur whose death in early middle age doomed the project. Years later, an elderly woman, reared in the rough Dakota ranch country, wrote what she really felt about Oelrichs and his upper class friends:

> These men lived different lives from the rest of us, and they did not fit into our homes very well. For that reason we had little to do with them. They constantly brought well-educated men into their homes and some women, too, who tried to establish interest in art, music, science and literature, which most of us had not learned to understand. Some of their guests constantly carried notebooks ... to take notes on everything they saw. Now, I understand what they were doing.
>
> Then I thought they were snooping on us. As I sit here now, I often wonder how this country would have developed if Mr. Oelrichs' health had held out. But that book is closed, I guess.

Indeed, it is—gone with the young Ivy Leaguers of the last century. But their impact is still felt in Colorado. On the Continental Divide are fourteen thousand-foot peaks named for Harvard, Princeton and Yale.

✦

CHAPTER 4

As a Phoenix Rising
from the Ashes

The title remittance man was coined in Australia, where many a second son spent his pittance on a simplistic life of pleasure and escape, leaving unanswered the letters of sisters and mothers begging him to come home.

With its relaxed value system, Australia often reinforced his insight into England's hypocrisies. No greater example of this phenomenon could be demonstrated than the tale of a second son that has its genesis in the tiny hamlet of Hollingbourne.

Tourists passing through Maidstone in Kent, southeast of London, are often searching for Leeds Castle, a magnificent structure so old it was rebuilt in 1280 and later expanded by Henry VIII in the sixteenth century. It is quite beautiful.

But few travelers go on from the castle to Hollingbourne, only another seven miles away, because it is strictly rural, a village of eleven hundred people. Yet in its modest way it is a treasury of the past—an historic gem with many facets.

Hollingbourne is on the south face of the North Downs of Kent. You reach it by rail or road, often penetrating forests whose large oaks and other deciduous species overarch the roadway and turn the journey into a succession of green tunnels. Finally, the road opens into Hollingbourne, which once was on the Pilgrim's

Way between Canterbury and Winchester. The pathway is marked in places by rows of sturdy yews, and a visit to the parish church validates the antiquity of its stones.

Architecturally, the church is beautiful in its simplicity. Unlike other places in Britain where building stones are gray and lifeless, the stones of Hollingbourne—and its parish church—are buff, almost honey-colored. Its builders incorporated ancient Roman tiles in the bell tower, making the church—itself five hundred years old—scarcely a fourth the age of these components.

The interior is no less lovely. The walls display memorials to important members of families who worshipped here over the centuries. The chief attraction is a velvet altar cloth almost ten feet long, a tribute to the age of faith.

When Sir John Culpepper went into twelve years of exile in France with Charles II, fleeing the Roundheads, his four daughters painstakingly embroidered the cloth as a show of their devotion. One daughter is said to have lost her sight during those years of minuscule stitching. Although it hangs behind protective glass, the tapestry's figures have darkened with age.

But if tiny Hollingbourne's history is rooted in the evolution of modern Britain, two of its historic manor houses nevertheless produced families whose restless descendants helped name major communities in North America. One is Greenway Court, a mansion of good account, which in the mid-1700s came into the possession of Thomas, Lord Fairfax, whose mother was a Culpepper. He migrated to the New World and gave his name to the city of Fairfax, Virginia.

Greenway Court is gone, replaced by a modern farmhouse, but the manor house of the second, lesser-known family still stands. It is Hollingbourne House, ancestral seat of the Duppas, who also have impressive memorials in Hollingbourne Church. Unlike the aristocratic Culpeppers, the Duppas were only landed gentry. But they prospered for hundreds of years, and one of their clan, Brian Philip Darell Duppa, christened the largest city in the American West, Phoenix, Arizona.

The Duppas originated in the borderland between England and Wales. For centuries, shrewd Welshmen migrated to the

Thames Valley to make their fortune. Baldwin Duppa (1640–1737) evidently was one of them, arriving in 1675 to become a prosperous storekeeper at the Royal Navy base at Chatham, on the Thames Estuary. Investing in land at Hollingbourne, ten miles southeast, he soon was wealthy enough to turn his heirs into gentlefolk.

Baldwin erected Hollingbourne House, the family seat, on a hill above the village in about 1700. The Duppas survived there for generations—in fact until the last Duppa died childless in 1971. The manor house still stands, a rectangular structure of fitted beige stones. A fierce gale struck the estate in the 1980s. Its landscaping was heavily damaged and still shows the effects. But the current owner, a businessman who designs and installs music systems, has made steady improvements.

While one of Baldwin Duppa's relatives had served as bishop of Chichester, Salisbury and Winchester and in 1775 authored *Guide to the Penitent*, the nineteenth-century Duppas were less pious. They still had their own private pew in the parish church, beneath a carved stone memorial to the bishop. But it's likely their thoughts were less on religion than on their own economic outlook in a period of low farm prices.

Like other gentry the Duppas found the Industrial Revolution a difficult time. Counties like Yorkshire, which had coal as well as sheep, tended to prosper but farmers in other areas were less successful. As long as income met outgo a landed family could make the ancient system of primogeniture work. But family obligations grew into heavy burdens as farm income dwindled. The growing labor forces of the big industrial centers demanded cheaper food, which suppliers provided by boosting their meat and grain imports. This, in turn, lowered prices received by the country squire and his tenants. The heir who bore the brunt of this downturn was Baldwin Duppa Duppa (that's correct: he honored two branches of the family by taking a double name) who became squire of Hollingbourne House about 1800. He and his wife, Mary Gladwin, had eleven children to ease over the bumps to careers and marriage. He solved the problem by borrowing, and then borrowing some more—in fact, he borrowed until he died in 1847.

In a strange elliptical way his financial distress contributed later in the century to the naming of a tiny community in the western North American desert for a mythical bird in classical Greek literature, the Phoenix, which had the power to regenerate itself. Almost at the same time the Duppa estate underwent its own strange cycle of regeneration in ways Duppa Duppa couldn't have foreseen—or welcomed. Happily for the narrative, the family's next generation reverted its name to Duppa.

Baldwin's eldest son, Baldwin Francis Duppa Sr., had six children, one of whom was christened Brian Philip Darell Duppa. He was born October 9, 1832, a second son destined for the worldly life of a remittance man in New Zealand and the Arizona Territory.

Inheritance under primogeniture can be extremely simple, or its complexities can rival a game of golf played in a prairie dog colony. The Duppa experience tended toward the latter.

Baldwin Francis Duppa, Sr., nicknamed Frank, was aware of the debt problems he would assume as the eldest son. He also knew that three of his younger brothers were gentlemen wastrels. Like their father they went deeply into debt to indulge their hunting sports and other recreational pursuits.

Frank, by contrast, tried to save money by moving his growing family to France for several years—income from tenant rents at Hollingbourne went a good deal further on the continent.

This international exposure also opened Frank Duppa's eyes to the failings of British education. Even though he had attended prestigious Winchester and, briefly, Cambridge University, he realized their deficiencies. He was appalled by the flogging and bullying of public schools with their narrow emphasis on sports and the classics. His playboy brothers represented this failure. Their schools had taught them that work was beneath their standard as gentlemen.

Frank acted. The very youngest of the brothers, George, was bright and hadn't been spoiled—yet. Frank persuaded his father to send young George to the progressive multilingual school, Hofwyl, in Switzerland. Frank's action was to have profound effects on the family. George, in fact, eventually saved the estate.

Had Frank lived longer he might have preserved the estate through his own efforts and given his family a better start in life.

Even so, he had considerable impact on British public school policy. Trained in the law, he moved from France to London to pursue a career. He became an active reformer and organized a group to goad the British government into direct sponsorship of the British school system; it gained ground only slowly but achieved its objective later in the century.

Frank wasn't there to see it. He died of tuberculosis in 1840 when his second son, Darell, was but seven. With Grandfather Baldwin Duppa Duppa coping with the finances until his own death in 1847, Darell didn't get much formal education. He may have attended the University of Paris because his widowed mother returned to France after Frank's untimely death. Darell (who came to use his mother's maiden name Darell because her family was socially superior to the Duppas) probably would have attended Hofwyl had his father lived.

As heir, Darell's elder brother, called Franky to distinguish him from father Frank, received a brief exposure to Hofwyl but also was sent to Cambridge for a more conventional education. He was totally fascinated by experimental chemistry and finally moved to London to work closely with other scientists. This put the estate in the hands of the trustees; Franky made no effort to assume his tenant-for-life role when his grandfather died in 1847. The heirs now saw that bankruptcy for Hollingbourne was a real possibility. The spendthrifts were in a state of consternation.

All except one—Frank's youngest brother, George. Swiss schooling had given George the will to overcome genteel poverty by hard work. He bought shares in a British colonizing enterprise, the New Zealand Land Company, which entitled him to farmland when he reached New Zealand. In 1840 shiploads of immigrants dropped anchor in the superb harbor where Wellington today reigns as the capital and commercial hub of the nation. But in 1840 it was simply raw country, dry and hilly, on the south end of the North Island.

George and the other migrants got a rude welcome. The British government, heeding the pleas of missionaries, ruled that the land being offered by the corporation couldn't even be purchased from the native Maoris. A small war ensued but shrewd George skipped over to the South Island to become a squatter in the forested and fertile Nelson area—another Oregon with a bit less rain.

For the next twenty-three years George Duppa profited mightily from sheep, developing a huge property called St. Leonard's Station. He branched out to create a transport system to haul sheep, cattle and wool to England. He was unscrupulous and acquired a reputation for sharp practices. But at least he had a plan, which included bringing his young nephew, Darell, in as a partner. Darell seized the offer because his future in Britain was bleak. He knew classical literature and languages but little else.

There was little money for Darell—just enough to knock around the world a bit and go to New Zealand and work for his Uncle George. Unfortunately, Darell stopped in Australia for some time en route and, when he joined his Uncle George in New Zealand in 1854, he had become more mature but also more cynical. He was well on the way to becoming a remittance man. While he had shown ambition in school, by the time he joined George Duppa he had adopted the rest of the family's distaste for physical work.

His first two years working for George prompted the latter to write his sister this analysis:

> Darell has been working with me for some time. If he only showed more drive. He is now what I fear ... lacking in ambition or drive. [Later he said Darell was] amiable, generous and careless to a degree—without purpose or ambition in life ... not a person I should feel justified in entrusting my affairs to.

During the next few years George established Darell on a small part of his large grant—apparently with little result. Darell worked only sporadically. But 1863 became a year of decision for both of them. George sold his New Zealand properties for 100,000 pounds, an immense fortune in those times, equivalent to half a million dollars. He returned to England and Darell resumed his wandering through the New World, soon finding a permanent home in the brawling American frontier territory of Arizona. He farmed, prospected and learned to survive in the rough society of Prescott, a mining town in west central Arizona.

George returned home aiming at just one thing—to take Hollingbourne as his own! He began his campaign almost immediately. In 1864 he purchased adjacent properties as they became available, and by the early 1870s he was in the driver's seat. He had no claim on the estate other than his big bankroll, a counterpoint to the family's need to pay its debts.

Darell's older brother, Franky, had succeeded to the squireship when the grandfather finally died in 1847. He lived in London, where his chemistry research won him membership in the prestigious Royal Society and didn't pay any debts at Hollingbourne. He let the trustees respond to George's maneuvers and died in 1873. His death propelled Darell into a key position because the grandfather's will had listed Darell as tenant-for-life after Franky. Darell could have returned home to lay claim to the title. Had he done so he might have rallied the family to his side, but he was content to receive rents and legal fees from George, who now lived in Hollingbourne House. George got the property by paying the trustees' price of 40,375 pounds, most of which then went to Franky's widow.

George settled in and became squire of an expanding estate at Hollingbourne. At fifty-two he felt young enough to marry Alice Miles, twenty, and lead the kind of gentlemanly existence he'd dreamed about in New Zealand. He was a good politician and was elevated to high sheriff of Kent in 1875—a prestigious honor indeed for a man who had started as a younger son in a world of primogeniture.

For Darell, primogeniture worked exactly as it usually did for an unambitious young gentlemen. Unwilling to play a squire's role in a debt-ridden enterprise, he chose to remain in Arizona. But he happily took George's regular remittances (sent until the transfer was completed) and led his Arizona drinking pals on regular two-day binges—or until the money ran out.

It would be unfair to seize on his drinking and his long periods of reclusive withdrawal as signs of failure. In fact, his twenty-seven years in the hot Southwestern desert were productive ones, and Arizonans owe him much. He gave them the names of two of their major cities.

Because of Darell's appearance and accent, Arizonans invented a good many myths about his origins and didn't hesitate to call him Lord Duppa, although landed gentry like the Duppas held no aristocratic titles. But anywhere in the West, when an Englishman got off a stagecoach with good clothes and a cultured accent, he was automatically labeled lord—sometimes out of respect, sometimes as an insult.

Darell Duppa was a drifter and descendant of a landed family near Maidstone. This younger son was sent to New Zealand to seek his fortune in sheep ranching. Failing this, he settled in Arizona and became an Indian fighter and land promoter. Arizona honors him today as the well-educated Englishman who named Phoenix and Tempe and helped establish irrigation farming in that area.

But those who disparaged him publicly usually found themselves in a fistfight. In time, Darell dressed in blue denim like other frontiersmen. Prospecting along Williams Creek near mile-high Prescott, he was attacked by Apaches and suffered an arrow wound in one arm. He soon learned to fight back.

There are blank spots in Darell's Arizona years, but his appearance is not one of them. Photos and contemporary descriptions show he was five feet ten or eleven inches tall, lanky, without an ounce of excess flesh. A flat, wide-brimmed hat topped his long dark locks, flawed complexion and handlebar mustache. This portrait disintegrated to a seedy appearance when he had been drinking—which was often.

Darell soon established a reputation as the best-educated man in the territory. He carried a well-worn library with him and could recite Shakespeare by the hour. But he also was a frontier renaissance man, ready to give intelligent advice or grab a rifle to defend against the Apaches. He was also a valuable addition to one of the most successful land promotions in western history.

With prices of grain, vegetables and other foodstuffs soaring because of the boom in Arizona's mining camps, a party from Wickenburg, not far from Prescott, went to the Salt River Valley in 1867 to organize an irrigation project. The party hoped to make a killing by raising vegetables and other produce for the rapidly expanding populations of the mining camps.

Darell went along, probably with some misgivings because of the enterprise's leadership. Jack Swilling, the chief promoter, was a tricky adventurer and swindler. But Darell had seen enough frontiers—both British and American—to know you can't always choose your friends. Swilling at least knew what he was after. As a hay hauler for federal forts in central Arizona, he had hatched a dream of irrigating the Salt River Valley. Ancient Indian ditches, long abandoned, snaked through the brush and cactus-covered desert surface. If those ditches had once grown crops, why not again?

Officially, Darell went along as secretary of the corporation, but a contemporary described him as the major domo of the camp from which Swilling administered the irrigation project. Darell was present when a name change was proposed for the first settlement south of the river, called Hayden Mills. With his background in classical history, Darell suggested Tempe, a vale in Greece celebrated by the ancients for its beauty. His proposal may have risen from wishful thinking but prophetically it was a miracle.

The Swilling party next located on the ruins of an ancient Indian settlement, just north of today's Sky Harbor International Airport. The leaders of the promotion gathered on a new ditch bank to discuss a name for their town. Swilling, a Southerner, wanted to call it Stonewall (after Confederate General Stonewall Jackson), but one of his partners, a Northerner, disagreed. A proposal to name it Salina was soon rejected because the word means "salt marsh," scarcely appealing to farmers.

Then, according to one account, Darell spoke up: "Let me suggest a name. This canal was partly built in a time forgotten now. Prehistoric cities, now in ruins, are all around you … let the new city arise from the ashes of these ruins. Let us call the city that is to be built Phoenix." His proposal was accepted.

Darell's work as secretary entitled him to settle on 160 acres served by the ditch, apparently at a reduced price of 750 dollars although some settlers were charged 10,000 dollars. Because the old Indian ruins made farming impossible, the land ownerships were moved four miles to the west—very close to the center of today's downtown Phoenix—and the land titles transferred.

Darell made sure that his designation, Phoenix, was transferred to the new location. A few irrigated vegetable crops were grown the first year, and the valley, as history records, grew into a cornucopia of fruit, vegetables and general farms. Even ostriches were raised for their feathers in a few decades.

But Darell had other arrows in his quiver. For reasons that are hard to fathom he established and operated the Agua Fria stage station between Phoenix and Wickenburg. Why did he choose such a remote and Godforsaken site? Some said he'd had a brush with the Apaches at Agua Fria and settled there to show them he was boss. Evidently, there was a demand for lodging and meals there and Darell served that demand. Some travelers reported the station was comfortable, but a later visitor was appalled, describing its location as uncompromising cactus-covered desert. Said a traveling author, John G. Bourke:

The dwelling itself was nothing but a "ramada" ... a roof of branches; the walls were of rough, unplastered wattle work of the thorny branches of the ironwood, no thicker than a man's finger, which were lashed by thongs of rawhide to horizontal slats of cottonwood; the floor of the bare earth, of course [—that went almost without saying in those days—] and the furniture rather too simple and meager ... a long unpainted table of pine ... served for meals or gambling, or the rare occasions when anyone took into his head to write a letter. This room constituted the ranch house in its entirety. Along the sides were spread piles of blankets, which about midnight were spread out as couches for tired laborers or travelers. At one extremity a meager array of Dutch ovens, flat irons, and frying pans revealed the "kitchen" presided over by a hirsute, husky-voiced gnome, half-Vulcan, half-centaur, who, immersed for most of the day in the mysteries of the larder, at stated intervals broke the silence with the hoarse command: "Hash pile, come a runnin." Rifles, pistols, belts of ammunition, saddles, spurs and whips ... lined the walls and covered the joists and cross beams. ... To keep them out of the sand-laden wind, which blew fiercely down from the north when it wasn't blowing with equal fierceness from the south, or west, or east, strips of canvas or gunny sacking were tacked on the inner side of the cactus branches.

Ultimately Darell returned to Phoenix and, having sold his farm, wandered a good deal and, according to police records, won a street fight in 1880 and was arrested for drunkenness later that year.

He was living with Dr. Oliver J. Thibodo when he died January 29, 1892, at age fifty-nine. He left a will giving Dr. Thibodo his share of the estate, which amounted to almost nothing. The only certain beneficiary was Darell's favorite saloon keeper, J. H. W. Jensen. He was willed Darell's gold watch.

His death brought kindly reminiscences. A friend, Art Ferrer, wrote, "He was independent, and apparently would tolerate no opposition but, except for his brushes with Indians, he is not known to have turned on anyone in anger. He was open-hearted and generous." That phrase echoes his Uncle George's assessment 40 years earlier that he was "amiable and generous."

A newspaper notice of his burial in Phoenix catches the spirit of many a remittance man: "He was a man of more than ordinary ability, polished and highly educated. He made few acquaintances, and he took more real pleasure out of life when alone in some secluded spot with his favorite English newspapers and the works of standard authors."

Like so many others of this breed, Darell was a loner. Had he married and had a family he might have left Phoenix a legacy of wise leadership plus heirs who, under American law, would have shared equally in his estate. Imagine the value today of 160 acres in downtown Phoenix.

Remittance men seldom married, they drank too much and they were torn between two worlds, one beyond the seas and, because of pride, beyond their reach, and the other not quite acceptable as home. Rejected by Britain's strict caste system, they still clung to it in quiet desperation as the value system that made them forever gentlemen. They bore the family's burden of failure.

An Australian poet, Judith Wright, wrote with great sensitivity about a disinherited remittance man sent to the "country of the scapegoat." (In biblical times the sins of the people were placed on the head of a goat that then was sent away into the wilderness bearing away the blame of others.) The country could be Australia or New Zealand—or Arizona.

Her concluding lines shift the scene from the desert back to England:

> That harsh biblical country of the scapegoat closed its magnificence finally round his bones polished by diligent ants. The squire, his brother, presuming death, signed over the documents, and lifting his eyes across the inherited garden, let a vague pity blur the formal roses.

That vague pity in Britain was the fate of so many remittance men who died in far-off places. It was typical of the times. The black sheep often wasn't even mentioned, and nieces and nephews barely knew of his existence. It is different for Darell—at least in Phoenix, where they now are proud of him.

By 1921 the pioneer plot in which Darell was buried in downtown Phoenix had fallen into vandalized disrepair, with hoboes using the wooden grave markers to stoke their cooking fires. He was reburied beneath a near-anonymous standarized marker in a conventional cemetery. In 1991, civic groups made amends: They moved his remains back to Pioneer and Military Memorial Park, a much-improved and a fitting place for pioneers. Phoenix realized that a man who could inspire them to dreams of ancient Greece and the continuity of history was as important to their progress as real-estate developers—perhaps more so.

✤

Jolly Good Advice for a Bartender

Every Western town of any size had a remittance man. There was one here in Salida who was well educated. He was friendly with a bartender who was having trouble paying off a loan from a local bank. One day the remittance man was sitting at the bar and saw his friend refuse to accept payment for a drink because the patron was offering some nearly worthless scrip issued by the same bank. The remittance man stepped in and advised him, "That may not be worth much to some people but why don't you take all you can get and pay off your loan?"

And that's exactly what happened.

—*Interview of Steve Frazee*

❧

CHAPTER 5

His Lady for a Tiger

It was a crisp autumn night in 1875 and the three-hundred-room great hall of Packington, surrounded by thousands of acres of forest and farmlands almost in the center of England, lay in total darkness. The soft bleat of restless sheep could be heard across the undulating Warwickshire plain. But the man standing quietly at the edge of the woods appeared to be waiting for a signal as he peered across the broad lawns that led to the dark bulk of the mansion.

Suddenly there was a hesitant flicker. A gleam from a first floor window quickly penetrated the darkness—the steady glow of a candle.

The man moved toward the light. He knew Packington. A year earlier he had been among the guests when the youthful seventh earl of Aylesford staged one of the social events of the year—a profligate, prodigious party in honor of the Prince of Wales, his friend who, in 1902, would succeed his mother, Queen Victoria, as ruler of Great Britain and India. A temporary pavilion had been erected to accommodate the visiting nobility at the party. Money flowed out of the earl's coffers like the champagne, band music, fireworks and dress balls he lavished on his many guests.

But now, in the darkness of the English Midlands, the visitor was on a different mission. The seventh earl of Aylesford, endowed with a great estate but little common sense, had left his beautiful wife, Edith, to go hunting tigers in India with the Prince of Wales.

The man hurried toward the candle held by Edith, the young countess, as she stood in the French doors looking out from the mansion's music room. The candle meant that the servants were in bed. Seeking out a darkened doorway, the man let himself in. What had begun as a court flirtation was now a torrid love affair, and Edith quite literally had given him the keys to Packington Hall. Soon the lovers were in each other's arms.

Thus did George Churchill, eldest son of the seventh duke of Marlborough and uncle of the infant Winston Churchill, trigger one of England's great Victorian scandals. He had met Edith on numerous occasions. Like other young women she was impressed, aware that as Marquess of Blandford he would succeed to his father's title and possession of magnificent Blenheim Palace. But his image of power and wild charm were a mask: The family was not as wealthy as it seemed and George was unstable. He had been expelled from Eton. Although he was married and the father of three children (Edith had two children), he was a womanizer. Edith was not the first.

The affair soon was out of hand. Victorians could tolerate boudoir hopping by married gentlefolk as long as it was done in secret. The servants must never find out because that meant the public would soon would be savoring the rumor-spiced details. At thirty-one, George was several years older than Edith and should have been wary. He wasn't and neither was she. When she stood in the doorway signalling her paramour, wax drippings from her candle fell on the sill. Seemingly a small thing, the servants later were to testify about this tell-tale stain as evidence that she had welcomed George in her husband's absence.

The love affair blossomed into an announcement by the couple that they planned to elope, seek divorce or separation and leave the children with relatives. Like most aristocratic scandals, the George-Edith relationship long would echo as gossip and in public print. Even today, decades later, the Right Honorable Charles Ian Finch-

Knightley, the current and eleventh earl of Aylesford, describes the events with an economy of words as he takes a visitor across the carpet of the mansion's lovely first-floor music room. He says:

> This is the doorway where she held the candle. The servants noticed candle grease on the floor by these French windows night after night. They told the agent [manager of the estate] and he kept watch and caught them at it.

One account says the steward also found George's tracks in the snow, adding to the mounting evidence that ripped the family apart, dragged their aristocratic name in the mud of adultery and even caused cabinet worries about the royal succession. Looking across the lovely landscape of his five thousand-acre estate, the present earl speaks slowly as he muses about the affair: "There was that one terrible thing—Blandford [George] and Edith ... there was a child by Blandford ... born in Paris and handed over, fostered, by a French family called Blount. He [George] was a damned fellow."

The latter is no mild epithet. In the earl's quiet words one senses great family pride going back to the reign of Henry VIII, when his ancestors acquired lands yielded through dissolution of the monasteries. His damning of George, the future duke of Marlborough, carries the weight of centuries.

Edith wrote to her husband in India saying that she planned to elope to Paris with George and that she would leave the children with her mother-in-law. This was a catalyst for a series of interlocking personal disasters that came close to destroying the Prince of Wales. Later historians obliquely skirted it as "an amorous affair," although the *London Times* used columns of type to report the lurid events that drove Edith to disgrace and her husband to an early grave as a hard-drinking Texas rancher.

This change of scene is improbable. England and Texas in the nineteenth century were as distant socially as they were geographically. But time was the arbiter: Two events occurred in 1849 that ultimately intersected to make the west Texas city of Big Spring the final backdrop for a shabby international intrigue involving not only great aristocratic English families but the

Prince of Wales, the future King Edward VII. On February 21, 1849, a first son was born on an estate near Coventry to the sixth earl of Aylesford. If ever a child was born with a silver spoon in his mouth it had to be this one, christened Joseph Heneage Finch, the seventh earl of Aylesford. There was the estate in Kent, and surrounding the family's historic Packington Hall were some twenty thousand acres of the best farmland in the English Midlands. As eldest son, young Joseph had much to inherit.

Later that same year on October 3, a celebrated American explorer, Captain Randolph B. Marcy, led an Army detachment

Joseph Heneage Finch, the seventh earl of Aylesford, stands far left on the porch of Packington Hall with the Countess of Aylesford and friends Prince Edward VII and the Princess of Wales. (Photo courtesy of Heritage Museum, Big Spring, Texas.)

across the mesquite-covered plains of west Texas to a rare large, natural spring. It was twenty yards square and fifteen feet deep and its fresh flowing water had attracted men and animals for millennia. In all directions a litter of bones and arrowheads testified to its attraction as a place where Indians ambushed wild animals coming to drink. In so arid a country such a waterhole was precious, and Marcy's report encouraged railroad engineers to use this route for a new rail line ordered by Jay Gould, the New York financier.

How Marcy's unusual spring intertwines with the life of an earl of Aylesford rests on an explanation of Victorian attitudes. In Texas, men might be equal, but in Britain the upper classes still ruled. In an era when France was throwing off the yoke of aristocracy and English adventurers were using guns, tools and their intelligence to conquer the world's deserts and jungles, Britain was locked in a time capsule. Laboring men were less than human, and servants provided the comforts and privileges that the estates had passed from father to eldest son for hundreds of years. But the Victorians cared about appearances: Private morality was one thing; letting the servants or public find out about it was quite another. Young Joseph was nurtured in this life of privilege, along with two younger brothers. Quickly surpassing a height of six feet he was initiated at seventeen into the masculine skills of horsemanship, shooting and archery. Although a heavy man he was excellent at polo. But his family also prepared him socially to succeed to the earlship. They sent him to Eton and Oxford and secured for him such civil posts as magistrate and deputy in County Warwick.

Except for the sports, his social life was uneventful until he met the beautiful Edith Williams, not of the nobility but from a good family. Her father, Pers Williams, was a respected member of Parliament. Romance blossomed and a wedding was set for January 10, 1871. But when the twenty-one-year-old heir learned that his father was dying, he advanced the wedding to January 8, a Sunday. He and Edith thus set the stage to become Lord and Lady Aylesford when the father died two days later. Hardly an occasion for a carefree honeymoon.

Had he stayed in the country Aylesford might have lived honorably as a stuffy rural aristocrat. But he and Edith joined

London society and moved quickly to the top. As members of the informal Marlborough House set they were part of a clique described as "His Royal Highness's friends and their wives," or perhaps more accurately as "some of His Royal Highness's mistresses and their husbands."

His Royal Highness, of course, was the Prince of Wales. The future king's affectionate nickname Teddy was a bit misleading; he was aware of his power and used it. And when his eye fell on the delectable Lady Aylesford, she apparently was nominated to join several other wives, including Jennie Churchill, mother of Winston, to brighten the Prince's romantic interludes.

Teddy's vicarious manipulation of his friends drew severe disapproval from his mother, Queen Victoria. But she had helped create the Marlborough set. When her beloved Prince Albert died in 1861 she withdrew from society in grief. The picture of Victoria wearing black became an icon of the last third of the century. The prince and his Danish wife, the beautiful Princess Alexandra, thus became the center of attention. Socially, they were the only game in town for young nobility—and the princess, in an alien setting, surrendered her husband to Victorian morality.

The prince played his social role to the hilt and displayed disturbing tendencies that lent danger to his friendships. He was, in fact, a rake whose gambling and boudoir-hopping were of great concern not only to Victoria but to Prime Minister Disraeli.

When trouble finally erupted in the George-Edith affair it soon involved George's capable and politically active younger brother, Lord Randolph Churchill, father of Winston. Lord Randolph was newsworthy not only because he was a member of Parliament but, like George, had grown up in famous Blenheim Palace, named for the battlefield in Bavaria where their ancestor, John Churchill, had distinguished himself against the French in 1704.

Seduction of another man's wife was not unusual in Victorian times. Aristocratic partners often sought such diversion after their first few children were born. But George was dangerous— playfully labeled a "wicked boy" by no less an authority than the Prince, himself. Scandal or not, George was drawn to a candle flame he couldn't resist.

The crisis escalated when it turned out that the Prince had written his own admiring letters to Lady Aylesford. Far from playing itself out or collapsing before family pressure, the love match flourished. Foolishly, the Prince encouraged it.

Also, the affair dovetailed with reports that Aylesford was romantically involved with a titled lady. By now Aylesford was known as Sporting Joe to his intimates who knew about his drinking and frequent forays into the dark streets of London in pursuit of prostitutes. He put Edith in a lonely position, vulnerable to George's advances.

Secretly enjoying what he was hearing, the Prince of Wales apparently didn't consider the consequences when he invited Aylesford to join his tiger hunting trip to India, which began in the autumn of 1875 and lasted well into 1876.

Through his machinations the prince had made two hearts grow fonder—but not Aylesford's. When the announcement of Edith's love for George reached India, Aylesford's enjoyment of a glorious hunting trip—with armies of Indian beaters driving tigers through the brush for the hunters to kill from the howdahs attached to the elephants—came to a sudden end. Edith and George had cuckolded him in public. He enlisted the aid of the prince who obligingly sent word by telegraph to London that George was "the greatest blackguard alive." A fuming Aylesford had his heavy rifle cleaned and made his slow way by elephant to the nearest railroad for the first leg of his long trip back to England. He said his goal was "to divorce and kill—in that order."

But Aylesford was forgotten for the moment because the Prince of Wales faced a personal crisis unwisely created by Lord Randolph who, in brotherly loyalty, was trying to pull George from the morass.

Lord Randolph had much to lose. His political star was rising and some saw him as a future prime minister. His ties to the prince were close: The prince in fact, had played a pivotal role in persuading the seventh duke of Marlborough to allow Lord Randolph to marry Jennie Jerome, the wealthy American commoner.

But the year now was 1876 and the prince, at thirty-four, was perilously close to exposure as a central figure in a public scandal partly of his own making, a scandal that was pitting him against his friends, including the Churchills and Lord Aylesford.

Arriving home, Aylesford found things still salvageable in terms of his own position, although Edith was out of reach. But when he threatened to divorce his wife, court nobility held its breath. Such a public step could bring the Prince of Wales into court as a witness, endangering his ascent to the throne.

Tensions escalated when Lord Randolph, who should have stayed tactfully on the sidelines, played the fool and secured the prince's indiscreet letters to Lady Aylesford. He showed them to the Princess Alexandra, the future queen of England. Ostensibly, he was enlisting Alexandra's help in heading off a divorce suit, but Alexandra (like her mother-in-law, Victoria) was not amused. The prince pursued defense of his honor by challenging Lord Randolph to a duel—a move that Churchill sidestepped by saying he would not lift his sword against his future sovereign.

The scandal persisted for several years. The prince silenced his friends by ostracizing the Churchills, announcing he would shun them and would refuse invitations from anyone who associated with them. Lord Randolph didn't immediately comprehend how neatly his throat had been cut. When he realized that he and Jennie were social pariahs, he cut his losses by accepting Prime Minister Disraeli's help in getting him appointed Lord Lieutenant of Ireland. Lord Randolph grumbled mightily, but he and Jennie booked passage for Ireland; their son, Winston, thus spent his early years in Dublin.

Aylesford tried to clear his name in an action for separation from Lady Edith but only dragged the affair deeper into the newspaper scandal columns. A queen's proctor investigated the case and uncovered Aylesford's "vulgar amours" with prostitutes in the unsavory Cremorne Gardens in Chelsea.

Next came the Dilke bombshell. The attorney general entered testimony that Sir Charles Dilke, whose castle was not far from Packington Hall, had been victimized and driven to drink by the intimacies between his wife and Lord Aylesford. The court officer observed that when Dilke killed himself on August 3, 1877, Lady Dilke that very night occupied Lord Aylesford's bed. The accuser didn't say his lordship was also in the bed but Victorian imaginations did the rest. Aylesford's life was in ruins.

Edith and George, now living in Paris as Mr. and Mrs. Spencer, had a child, but George's passion was cooling. He refused to marry her, and the child was illegitimate. George labeled Edith "a remarkable mistress but impossible as the future duchess of Marlborough." Like his younger brother, Lord Randolph, he finally married an American, the Widow Hammersley, who brought him a considerable dowry. While Aylesford may have suffered public obloquy, he finally secured court cancellation of Edith's alimony and she disappeared—a nonitem in the debris left by the scandal.

But Aylesford's private agonies continued. He drank heavily and often sought relief through numerous hunting trips. Among his trips were several to North America. Not much is known about them until he decided to quit England forever.

With his name now the subject of crude London jokes, he decided that America would be his new home. He launched the legalities such a step would involve. Having fathered only daughters, his inheritance would go to a nephew. The estate's lawyers agreed to give him 50,000 dollars annually if he left his family duties in England. This amount was only half of his income in Britain but it was lavish by American standards. There is some belief that he planned to invest on the American frontier to provide an estate for his two daughters.

But where should he go in America? The question was evidently answered by Jay Gould, whom Aylesford had met on a previous trip. Gould was building the Texas and Pacific Railway through West Texas and was familiar with the Big Springs area. He or his agents apparently persuaded Aylesford that here he would find opportunities in cattle ranching and that there would be ample wild game to satisfy "Sporting Joe's" instincts for the hunt. Aylesford showed up with an arsenal of rifles and shotguns and a retinue of servants and retainers. A short time later his younger brothers, Daniel Harry Finch and Clement Edward Finch, joined him for adventure and investment.

Stories about Aylesford's impact are legion, and no doubt some of them are true. He didn't immediately go to Big Spring. His first extended stop was in 1881 at Colorado City, Texas, where he sought out John Birdwell, a former Texas ranger who was recommended as a dependable contact. Debarking from the train, Aylesford found Birdwell and declared: "I am Joseph Heneage Finch, earl of Aylesford, seventh member of my illustrious family to bear the title." Birdwell reportedly eyed the impeccably dressed Englishman—who looked older than his thirty-two years—and said, "Look here, earl. All that stuff won't go down here. We'll just call you Judge, and in that way, nobody will get hurt." The tactic worked, although Birdwell in a moment of relaxed inhibition once introduced the Englishman as the Lord God Aylesford.

Birdwell provided Aylesford with a good deal of hunting, and during one of these forays Aylesford found land near Big Spring that appealed to him. His arrival there in the summer of 1883 brought on as much local titillation as it had at Colorado City. Rumor spread about his largesse. He reportedly bought twenty-three thousand acres of ranch land, according to some stories, and twice that much according to others. It seems likely he put money down on considerable land—and used it—but didn't pay off the mortgages. Gossip thrived on details of his personal life.

According to local historians, Aylesford arrived at Big Spring to find the Cosmopolitan Hotel fully booked and unable to accommodate his party. Asked what the hotel was worth, the manager named a price and Aylesford immediately purchased it for 4,000 dollars—more than it was worth.

The earl lived at this hotel occasionally, but built a wooden house on his ranch seventeen miles northeast of Big Spring, at the headwaters of Wild Horse Draw. Here he installed his hunting arsenal.

Like many Englishmen in America, Aylesford was bilked on commercial deals. He purchased several thousand head of cattle at book value—meaning they weren't counted. When he sold, the actual cattle number was so few the herd was almost valueless. He liked to spend money on liquor—for himself and for his friends. His cowboys loved "the jedge" for his fast draw with a whiskey bottle. One account says he purchased a saloon one evening, invited his friends to an all-night party, and sold the property back to its former owner the following day.

A newspaperman writing for a Chicago newspaper captured a graphic portrayal of Aylesford's life at Big Spring when he visited the earl's one-and-a-half-story ranch house and hunting lodge. The reporter described the exterior as plain and unpainted, but the walls of its nine rooms were covered with rifles, shotguns, handguns, cartridge belts, game bags and other hunting paraphernalia. The story appeared in Chicago and took special note of a pile of whiskey and beer bottles of haystack proportions beside the lodge. The reporter found a great variety of brands among the empties—but a strong preference for Scotch and Irish whiskey and English gin.

Disaster soon struck: Fire destroyed the lodge and its 137 weapons, among which were double-barreled rifles, custom-made for the Prince of Wales' shikar to India.

Aylesford seemed undaunted. He continued to buy drinks for his friends, but he separated his socializing from his commercial transactions. According to Big Spring author Joe Pickle, Aylesford did not give things away, rumor to the contrary: "While he sometimes lost property because he could not pay his debts he was not guilty of recklessly or impulsively giving it away. There was not, however, a stingy bone in his body as witness the many accounts of his liberality as a host, and particularly in buying drinks."

He was a perfect gentleman. While he had little contact with women he was "given to much bowing before the ladies," according to Pickle. And he bathed every morning, "even if he had to break the ice on the water."

But there was a darker side, too. When he returned briefly to London in 1884 to make provisions for his daughters by selling some property, he became involved in a row at a railroad station, in which he suffered a broken leg. More details are lacking.

Returning to Texas, he announced his permanent residency in the United States. But he seemed changed. His spirit was more subdued and he hunted less, only partly because his lodge and weapons had burned.

By December 1884, he abandoned trips to his ranch and kept to his quarters in the Cosmopolitan Hotel. But he continued to eat heartily and drink copious quantities of liquor. Records show he ordered twenty-five quarts of whiskey and gin on December 28 following a Christmas party. While he sometimes played a hand of euchre with his brothers, Daniel and Clement, and other members of his staff, he increasingly took to his couch.

On January 13, 1885, according to his physician, Dr. J. C. Utter, he put down his cards, arose from the table and declared, "Goodbye, boys."

Returning to his couch, he lay down, pulled up the covers and died peacefully. In the embalming process, according to Dr. Utter, his liver was found to be "hard as a rock." The death certificate listed cirrhosis as the cause of death.

His English valet accompanied the body back to Britain. Press reports called him a "a boon companion to the Prince of Wales" and said the prince was "much affected" by Aylesford's sudden death.

Perhaps. But it's a fair conclusion that he had firmer friends among the rough Texans than he had at home. They may have approached the strange British aristocrat with amusement, but they treated him as an equal and that may have been their greatest gift—a friendly way of showing respect for him as a person. The sincerity of their remembrance even today tinges Big Spring's pride in its history. In London's aristocratic circles he was a joke; in Texas he was considered an eccentric but intelligent and decent—and that's all frontiersmen asked. It's too bad his confused wife couldn't have joined him in Texas. But in the end it was pride—stubborn, aristocratic British pride—that destroyed them both.

The eleventh earl of Aylesford has a few disagreements with the stories told in Texas:

> Our story about his buying the hotel is that he said: 'I want your best room' and when the owner said he had no space Aylesford said: 'What is your best price for the hotel' and he [the owner] gave it. So he bought the hotel.

> We agree with all that, except the size of the staff of retainers [some stories have said he brought a retinue of 30]. That I disagree with. He couldn't have had that many. But the rest I agree with. And he died in that first room he occupied in the hotel.

But the eleventh earl believes his predecessor's heavy drinking and bizarre conduct in Texas were "unintentional—he was so generous with his money that I think he was egged on by the locals … but having said that I think he died of drink." And asked if the Aylesford's experiences in England had been so bitter he did not want to live, the eleventh earl continues: "I think that's right."

Still carrying the full title of the Right Honorable Charles Ian Finch-Knightley, eleventh earl of Aylesford, the present earl also holds the largely ceremonial title of Lord Lieutenant of the County of West Midlands, which has more than 3.5 million people. But at seventy-three he has given over management of the estate to his son, Charley—his heir who holds the traditional provisional title of Lord Guernsey. His children have given him five grandsons among nearly a dozen grandchildren, which should carry the family title far into the twenty-first century.

While his son supervises the tilling of the land the earl takes special interest in the estate's large herd of black fallow deer, which are culled and sold each year, and on the fine pheasant crop that produces excellent hunting in the fall. He said his custom-made shotguns are old "but they should just about see me out." And he still reminisces about the family's troubled past. He related a coincidence in the death of Edith's bastard son. Reared in France by the Blounts, his foster family, the son joined the French Army on the Western Front. In close contact with a British unit he recognized the Aylesford name and hunted up Michael Aylesford, cousin of the present earl. The two soldiers had a brief reunion but subsequently were killed on the same day.

❧
_____

A Ranch Pilgrim at Work

Being a description of a young British remittance man at work on a ranch in Alberta in the 1880s:

"Cynicus" joined the party and took charge of the saddle ponies. He was a "pilgrim" who had gone through English school life and was now in training for ranch life, assisted by an annual remittance of 100 pounds. He gave his work in exchange for his board and instruction. His saddle horses were supplied. He provided his own saddle, according to the usual custom. He was not what is known as a paying ranch pupil; that is, he did not pay for the privilege of working. His remittances came in half yearly, and were often anticipated quite a while in advance. He was not of the "wild and woolly" sort, just a trifle free on occasional trips to the town, which were followed by a day or two of contrition.

During these seasons of penitence he would give vent to his feelings by expressing in strong adjectives his thoughts concerning the unaccountable ease with which his money had parted from him, and the deplorable physical condition in which he found himself. He was at times given to adverse criticisms of the country, the climate and everything in general. From the frequency of these cynical moods he came to be dubbed "Cynicus" by his cowboy companions, and the name stuck to him. Notwithstanding this, from having a splendid physique, and being a good all-round athlete, accompanied by a good-natured gentlemanly bearing, he had what these qualities will always command, the respect and goodwill of the cowboys.

... There has been unsparing criticism of what is termed the injustice of bringing young fellows from the old country to the ranch and charging them for their education. It is contended that the work given by the pupil should be ample compensation for his board and any instruction he receives.

My experience has proved that on a cow ranch the average youth, or any youth, from the old country will, during the first year or two, fail to see, through inexperience, where loss could easily have been prevented, and he would not have known how to prevent it if he had observed danger, besides the occasional mistakes made while performing the routine of multifarious duties.

The cattle ranch earns what it receives for instructing the ranch pupil and the ranch pupil usually receives full value for the amount paid in the experience he gains.

—John R. Craig
Ranching with Lords and Commons

✤

CHAPTER 6

The Man
Who Would Be King

If the state of Wyoming marches to a different drummer—
if it has in its soul a sort of Alice-in-Wonderland disbelief in the
natural order of things—blame it on Moreton Frewen, a British
blueblood who spent hundreds of thousands of pounds of other
people's money to transform northeastern Wyoming into a
nineteenth-century cattle kingdom with himself as king. He
almost succeeded.

There is no single phrase—or an entire phrasebook—that
could possibly describe fully this strange man who was born
twelve years before Lewis Carroll wrote *Alice in Wonderland*.
The two characters should have been linked: Moreton Frewen
could have been a perfect marching companion for Alice in her
other-worldly adventures.

Frewen was by turns brilliant, stupid, generous, selfish,
callous, loving, naïve, politically wise and politically inept. He
was a promoter of deals, and his vocabulary embraced the charm
and wit of Shakespeare's. But when he agreed to edit a book
written by his young nephew, Winston Churchill, the result was
a disastrous two hundred mistakes in spelling and usage. London
critics labeled it "A Mad Printer's Reader." Britain's future prime
minister was philosophical. He wrote to his mother, saying "As

71

far as Uncle Moreton is concerned, I now understand why his life has been such a failure in the city and elsewhere."

A younger son of a wealthy Sussex squire, Moreton was born May 8, 1853. He received a gentleman's education, which he found to be a very low hurdle. Even Cambridge failed to instill intellectual discipline, and he soon opted for wagering forays to the Newmarket races as a more interesting course of study. What labor he expended in school was reserved for polo and steeple-chasing. He hardly knew when his formal schooling ended, because his life moved effortlessly forward—wenching in the shires in summer, shooting grouse in the fall and gambling in the south of France if the British winter was severe.

Moreton Frewen, adventurer and Wyoming ranching pioneer, helped build the western cattle industry but died broke. A born promoter, his spelling errors shocked his nephew, Winston Churchill. (Photo courtesy of the Denver Public Library, Western History Department.)

But the time of reckoning came, as it usually did for young British gentleman who, as younger sons, had no estate to inherit. His Uncle Charles, upon whom he depended for an inheritance, died and left him nothing. A disappointed Moreton turned to cards and had a run of good luck until he decided to test his fortunes fully and with finality on the horses. He resolved to bet his entire future—on one race. If he lost, he determined to be off to America to seek his fortune as a cattle rancher in Wyoming. He put his money on Hampton in the Doncaster Cup on Friday the 13th, September 1878. Hampton lost, so Moreton cheerfully liquidated all his possessions and made plans to go to America.

An older brother, Richard Frewen, decided to join Moreton's American adventure. As sons of a second marriage, they had no expectations of land inheritance but each received a settlement of 16,000 pounds upon the death of their father, Thomas Frewen, in 1870. By 1878, Moreton was virtually bankrupt and it was Richard's 16,000 pounds that launched the Wyoming cattle venture. In other ways, too, Richard was a good man to have along. He had already explored the Kashmir and done mapping in Africa. They made an impressive pair of frontiersmen. Each was six feet three inches tall and each was an expert rider and hunter.

Of course, proper British gentlemen had to mix pleasure with business, so the trip to Wyoming was arranged as a sporting foray, with four other gentlemen joining as huntsmen, armed with large bore African rifles, guns that were more than a match for any "savage" antelope or buffalo on the North American continent.

But leaving wasn't easy. Moreton's pursuit of pleasure had put him in the same fast social lane as the Prince of Wales, who, two decades later, in 1901 would become King Edward VII upon the death of his mother, Queen Victoria. In fact, Moreton and the prince shared the same mistress, actress Lillie Langtry, and now Moreton had to say goodbye. The farewell with the actress took longer than expected, but he finally presented her with the gift of his favorite carriage horse and bolted for the point of departure, Liverpool. Chartering a special train, he raced to the seaport where Richard and the other hunters were already aboard the

Bothnia, departing the harbor for New York. Engaging a tender, Moreton caught up with and boarded the *Bothnia* at sea.

No wonder he never had enough money.

The hunting in the Big Horn mountains north of Rawlins, Wyoming, was superb, and by late December the Frewens' companions had their fill and went home. But the Frewens, with two local guides, set out eastward for the Powder River area in a foolhardy search for ranch land in blizzard country. The snow came and it was only through the cleverness of one of their guides, Jack Hargreaves, known as a good frontier type, that they surmounted the last pass to the Powder River.

Hargreaves stampeded a herd of buffalo through the pass, flattening the deep snow sufficiently to allow their horses and mules to follow. The desperate gamble paid off. In a bend in the river beyond, the Frewens discovered exactly the site they wanted for their base of operations.

First, they bought land for a homestead, called it Big Horn Ranche and built an uncommonly large two-story cabin, the largest "log castle" the territory was to see for many years. Then they sent out word they were in the market to buy cattle. Their theory was simple. Once settled on their wooded, well-watered home ranch they could turn an infinite number of cattle loose to graze the open public range. The more cattle one had the more the herd multiplied, the lower the unit cost (perhaps as little as 70 cents per animal in maintenance per year) and the more the profit. The Frewens claimed that their range, mostly public land, and covering most of northeast Wyoming, equaled Ireland in size.

But even a core herd for an operation that size took more money than the Frewens had, so Moreton began a nearly endless quest for liquidity through the sale of shares in the Frewen Brothers Ranch Company in New York and London. More than cattle was involved: Moreton's traveling lifestyle was extravagant. He spent lavishly to entertain wealthy Britons who might become investors. Desiring a staging area in Cheyenne, where wealthy cattlemen congregated, he joined the prestigious Cheyenne Club, which catered not only to Wyoming land barons but rich American and British adventurers arriving aboard Union Pacific trains, and built a charming guest house a few blocks from the club for his convenience and for entertaining guests bound for Powder River.

Slowly, Moreton raised the money from all the sources he could find, including his friends. Hugh Lowther, an heir to the Lonsdale fortune, had been a guest at Powder River and as a result took a gamble which became a near-disaster. Lowther was twenty-two and his brother, St. George Lowther, twenty-four, the fourth earl of Lonsdale, was already proprietor of the one hundred thousand-acre English estate worth 16 million dollars. Hugh was next in line but saw his chances of inheritance as practically nil because the law of primogeniture would bypass him and give the estate to St. George's son, should there be one. But he was caught up enthusiastically in Moreton's cattle scheme and plunged ahead. He needed quick cash.

So he sought out a society moneylender named Sam Lewis and sold him his "contingent reversionary interest" in the Lonsdale estates for 40,000 pounds. To Lewis it was a bet with long odds (maybe one hundred to one) that Hugh would inherit the estate. But should he do so, Lewis would get a return of far more than 40,000 pounds, perhaps a return of forty to one on Hugh Lowther's share of the inheritance. Hugh got the money and promptly invested all of it in Frewen Brothers.

A strange series of events then unfolded. St. George learned of his brother's rash act and urged the Lonsdale trustees to buy back the reversion from Sam Lewis, which they did. St. George died three years later at age twenty-seven, without a son. Hugh Lowther became the fifth earl of Lonsdale but the trustees, not surprisingly, withheld the estate from Hugh's grasp. He did, however, receive 80,000 pounds annually as the estate's life tenant, a rather opulent income that enabled Hugh to regard his Frewen Brothers shares as a fairly innocuous bad debt.

But if Britons investing in ranching shares were gullible so were British gentlemen buying cattle. There is a common story about Moreton's first cattle purchase from Tim Foley. Foley was a southern Wyoming rancher who reputedly took advantage of Moreton's naïveté by driving his herd around a small hill twice for the purchase count, thus doubling the price the Frewens paid for the herd. It probably is untrue, because Moreton hired competent foremen, such as the redoubtable Fred Hesse. Men of such competence wouldn't have fallen for such a stunt. Besides, he also got the Foley 76 brand. (Virtually the same story is told about other Britons in Canada, Colorado and Texas, suggesting a frontier eagerness to snicker at the British.)

But not even Fred Hesse could protect so vast a territory from rustlers and winter storm loss, both of which cut deeply into profits. Frewen redoubled his efforts to raise money, making dozens of trips across the Atlantic in the few years that he ran the Big Horn Ranche.

With his elegant charm and store of adventure stories he was welcome at dinner parties anywhere, and it was in New York City that the millionaire yachtsman, Leonard Jerome, welcomed Moreton to his household. Jerome's wife and daughters spent a good part of each year socializing in England and on the continent. One day Moreton had tea at the Jerome mansion, 25 Madison Square. There he met Jerome's daughter, Clara. At twenty-nine she was a slightly shopworn beauty who was much aware that her younger sister, Jennie, had married extremely well to Lord Randolph Churchill and already had a five-year-old son, Winston. Worse, Clara's marital prospects in Britain had taken a nosedive through no fault of her own.

The fates which brought Clara and Moreton together sprang from a royal British scandal with undecurrents savage enough to damage careers and social standing for several noble families. It rankled deeply.

As detailed in the previous chapter, the scandal swirling about Lord and Lady Aylesford was abetted the Prince of Wales who seemingly encouraged their infidelities by inviting Aylesford on a lengthy trip to hunt tigers in India. But when the hot breath of London scandal pointed at the Prince's involvement, he was only too happy to divert attention to the Churchill (Marlborough) family. When Lord Randolph Churchill, who in happier times had received the Prince's blessing in his marriage to an American socialite, Jennie Jerome, sided with brother George against the Prince the whole Marlborough clan was ostrasized. Lord Randolph was lucky to salvage a minor appointment in Britain's Irish office, taking Jennie and Young Winston with him on a four-year exile to Dublin.

Clara felt the ostracism, also. With her London social ambitions at low ebb, she went home to New York, insuring her attendance at the Jerome function attended by Moreton Frewen. Frewen wooed and soon won Clara's hand in marriage. The wedding was a gilt-edged affair at Grace Episcopal Church, followed by a reception at Madison Square Garden. Clara was wearing a necklace with thirty large diamonds, the society columns noted.

The newlyweds took a short honeymoon up the Hudson River and then entrained for the West. Moreton tried to ease Clara's arrival in the rough West, stopping first at Cheyenne and then taking the Union Pacific to Rock Creek, jumping off place for Powder River. They had a rough ride in an old four-horse

Two American sisters who moved in high society in London. Jennie Jerome (left), wife of Lord Randolph Churchill, was mother of Winston Churchill. As a member of the Marlborough Set her life was dogged by scandal after Randolph died of syphillis. Clara Jerome (right) married Moreton Frewen in New York City when her London social life collapsed in the royal ostracism of the Churchills. Frewen built Clara a log "castle" in Wyoming, which they soon abandonded. (Photo courtesy of the Denver Public Library, Western History Department.)

coach and, at the first stage stop. Clara and her maid saw the West up close: dirty men constantly scratching themselves and wearing revolvers in their belts. There was the overpowering smell of roasting venison and other exotic dishes. Things brightened at the next stop, Fort Fetterman, where the commanding officer invited the Frewens to supper, at which his daughter sang piano solos for the honored guests.

Clara did her best with her log "castle," which contained a drawing room complete with a grand piano. They entertained a steady flow of prominent Americans and visiting British sportsmen and their wives.

But the rough life finally wasn't for Clara, especially after a miscarriage. She soon left for New York and then London—the two cities in which Clara and Moreton were to maintain a haphazard but loving marriage that had to be strong because it was beset by constant money problems. How much money Clara got from home isn't certain but it must have been considerable. They had two sons, Hugh and Oswald, and a daughter, Clare.

By making innumerable trips across the Atlantic, Moreton Frewen maintained a delicate balance between his Wyoming cattle enterprise and political and financial involvements in Britain. He could have stood for Parliament but decided against it. He worked Britain's upper crust for hundreds of thousands of pounds for the ranch. His ambitions for Frewen Brothers Ranch were boundless. At one point he built a slaughter and meat-storage facility next to the Union Pacific rail line atop Sherman Hill between Cheyenne and Laramie. The lofty installation was high enough and old enough to store meat with natural refrigeration. He theorized that he could sell meat more cheaply. The project failed.

In 1882, Moreton faced a serious crisis: Richard Frewen withdrew from the partnership after three years. He was going home and he wanted his money back. Moreton didn't have that much money, but neither did he want newspapers to air the rift and thus endanger his money-raising efforts. He determined to go public with a general stock sale. He did well, raising some 300,000 pounds for the venture he now called the Powder River Cattle Company Ltd., with its cattle continuing to carry the "76" brand the Frewens had made famous.

Moreton had some breathing room and plunged into cattle industry affairs on a transatlantic basis. He fought the meat packers and railroads and impetuously bought one thousand acres of land at Superior, Wisconsin, as a staging area so he could ship young Western cattle to Britain for finishing. With British farming capacity underutilized he theorized that fattening the animals in Britain would be profitable. The strategy was jury-rigged for political reasons. Frewen needed Canadian support and thus proposed transshipping the cattle from Wisconsin by way of Canada to win Canadian support for the venture.

The idea was clever and Wyoming gave Moreton semiofficial status to promote the project in London and Washington. He was welcomed in both the U.S. Senate and Britain's House of Lords. He was as charming as ever and won passage of some legislation but not enough. British farmers weren't going to allow their beef markets to be taken over by Americans. And the Beef Trust in Chicago, protective of its packing houses, reacted savagely. Even Fate was against Moreton. Just as he was lobbying hardest for British relaxation of import restrictions, word reached London that Texas fever, carried by ticks, had spread to the northern ranges where Moreton's cattle were. That provided the ammunition needed to defeat Moreton, keep his slaughter cattle from bypassing Chicago and keep his feeder cattle out of Britain.

Meanwhile, back at the ranch, his backers—like Richard—were becoming impatient with the lack of profits. They began to withdraw their support and dispose of their shares. Even Hugh Lowther, now the fifth earl of Lonsdale, backed away from his outspoken support, although he did not press to get his money back.

For a time, Moreton was a prisoner of his own success at raising money. As head of the firm, he contracted—as a show of good faith—to sell none of his own shares until 1887. That was disastrous. The winter of 1886–1887 was one of the worst in Western history, killing an estimated one million cattle. It triggered the slow conversion of open-range cattle operations like Moreton's to smaller outfits harvesting wild slough hay in the river valleys to carry their herds through starvation winters.

Having lost his shareholders' confidence, Moreton resigned from the company in 1886. One of his last managerial acts, however, was a wise one. In the fall of 1886 he saw how dry and overgrazed his ranges were and shipped part of the company's thirty-nine thousand cattle to Canada just in time to save them from icy starvation. Many of the rest perished. His investors had little left and Moreton was 150,000 dollars in debt. His family tried to help. A younger brother, Steven, scraped up 5,000 pounds, which he gave to Moreton.

Moreton had a few triumphs. One was to welcome Lillie Langtry to Cheyenne during her 1884 western stage tour in the cast of W. S. Gilbert's play, *Pygmalion and Galatea*. Prior to the performance, which was a sellout at the Cheyenne Opera House, Moreton took his old flame to a private supper at his Cheyenne guest house. He also left the West a wiser place in the marketing of its cattle. His struggle to bypass the middlemen was one that would go on for decades.

But his expectation of vast profits from cattle on the northern Wyoming ranges was far too optimistic.

He left a legacy of bitterness among newer Wyoming settlers because it was he who ordered the hanging of a cattle rustler in an event which became, in Owen Wister's masterpiece, *The Virginian*, a symbol of heartless cattle barons arrayed against small farmers and ranchers. Moreton had no trouble identifying with land barons. That's what his family had been for generations.

His Wyoming chapter closed, Moreton scraped together enough money from the family, plus unsecured borrowing from his old school friends, to buy a house in London, which he soon mortgaged. He gambled on horses and fought with his creditors. Through the influence of his brother-in-law, Lord Randolph Churchill, Moreton got a job as a financial adviser to the Nizam of Hyderabad in India at 500 pounds a year, plus expenses. He found Far East politics incredibly tortuous and quite beyond his scope. Besides, he still had money problems at home (including a lawsuit against his old employer, the Powder River Cattle Company Ltd.) and soon returned to London to promote other schemes—so desperately that he even tried to force his children to lend him their family birthright due from Clara's mother's estate after Clara died. Daughter Clare, being twenty-one, could mortgage that future income, and this was what Moreton was after.

Clare, who became a successful sculptress and journalist (and once claimed an affair with Charlie Chaplin that Chaplin denied), perhaps understood her father best. She said of him in a letter to her brother, Hugh, "He struggles on misguidedly, all for the best—oh my God what a 'best!' " Then she added, "Don't feel bitter, Hugh dear ... Providence put him in this world and gave him life. He has failed. Our lives are before us."

They helped their father as much as they could, but by this time none of them had much money.

Moreton's days of going back and forth between London and the United States were far from over, however. He involved himself in a newly patented ore-reduction mill in Cripple Creek, Colorado. The process didn't work and Moreton lost more money. He jumped into American politics to try to get the U.S. Mint to stamp out silver coins for Mexico—an obscure self-serving scheme that got the usual polite attention in Congress but no action. What he was really trying to do was corner the silver market. He promoted the St. Lawrence Seaway for its tidal power and shipping access decades before its time.

People tried to be sympathetic but he made it difficult. Many shrugged their shoulders and used his London nickname "Mortal Ruin." Had he deployed his various inheritances with care he could have been a benevolent and famous financier or politician. As it was he was a raffish character you lent money to at your peril.

Moreton's death in London in 1924 set off a spate of recollections of his adventuresome life. Biographers, recalling his sophisticated concepts of cattle marketing and his predictions of the Panama and Suez canals decades before they were built, put him down as a visionary. As one author said, "He scaled peaks from which he could see the El Dorado that later generations sometimes found but he did not." The clerk who accepted his will for probate didn't bother with such symbolism. He noted routinely on the document as he filed it, "Effects: under 50 pounds."

✤

How the Money Arrived

How did a remittance man or other British traveler get money from home in the late nineteenth century? It was easy, according to Simon Bennett, an archivist at Lloyd's Bank in London, one of Britain's largest banks.

As Bennett noted in a recent interview:

> It would be done through an agency, The sender would go to his or her branch of Lloyd's Bank (or some other bank) and transfer that sum. That branch would contact the head office of the bank—its foreign or colonial department—and then this department would telegraph the foreign agency, American, Canadian, Australian or whatever and they would credit that to their bank in the name of the party to draw the money. And he would have only to ask for it.

> The process would take perhaps less than a day. The recipient would receive cash or could build up an account. ... At the end of the year Lloyd's would settle the money out to the agency in bullion for all the numerous transactions in the last six months or a year.

> The agents in Canada might be the Bank of British North America or the Imperial Bank of Canada. A recipient could go into their branches. Others would have been Thomas Cook & Son, the Merchants National Bank of Boston, the Merchants Loan and Trust Companies Bank of Chicago, Drexel & Company, Philadelphia. In Australia, Thomas Cook and the Union Bank of Australia Ltd., the London Bank of Australia Ltd., the English-Scottish & Australian Bank Ltd., the Queensland National Bank Ltd., and the National Bank of New Zealand Ltd., would be available. There were similar agencies in Asia and other countries of the world.

82

❖

CHAPTER 7

Texans with a British Accent

Tall ironweeds pull at your elbows, grassburs cling to your clothing and goathead vines lie ready with vicious spikes to lock their seedheads to rubber-soled shoes or even pierce a woman's thin-soled sandal. The scene is in the Texas Panhandle, not far from the historic cowtown of Clarendon southeast of Amarillo. And your guide is Betty Boston, wife of a recent owner of the River Ranch of Alfred Rowe. Like most Texans she is proud of the Panhandle's British heritage, of which Rowe was a fine example.

Rowe was an Englishman. His cowboys called him Lord Rowe out of respect, although he was only a wealthy commoner. And while he ranched in the Clarendon area for only thirty-two years, he symbolized as much as anyone the powerful pull that lured thousands of Britons—shrewd investors, adventuring aristocrats and opportunity-seeking remittance men (sometimes a mix of all three)—to the Great Plains and changed its history dramatically.

From South Texas to the plains of the Dakotas and Alberta—and far to the West—it was called the cattle bonanza. But while the old Rowe Ranch still has the graceful lines of a competent nineteenth-century architect, the inevitable law of entropy is bringing on the disorder that comes to things untended, whether

Egyptian pyramids, paper airplanes or old ranch houses. The scene is like a funeral with an excess of pallbearers: Tall weeds and mesquite almost obscure the old house on the brush-choked bank of the Salt Fork of the Red River.

The ranch once bustled with the excitement of great profits being made on cattle. What stories its long front porch could tell about the days when rough cowhands and elegant English dandies sought its shelter from the sun. And what a sense of tragedy must have prevailed here on an April day in 1912 when word arrived of the sudden death of Alfred Rowe in the icy Atlantic Ocean.

Alfred Rowe, younger son of a worldly British mercantile family, pioneered the RO Ranch at Clarendon, Texas. He died in the sinking of the Titanic *when he refused to climb into an overloaded lifeboat, insisting he was a strong swimmer. (Photo courtesy of Paramount Publishing Company, Amarillo, Texas.)*

In fact, Rowe's death came near the end of the British era in Texas. Applying entropy to human economic history, the disorder, confusion and neglect brought on by World War I was in the wings. British investment in cattle would never regain its spontaneous vitality. But while it lasted it was wonderful and exciting.

And historic. That history is gauged by the comments of two men with a recollection of the open range. One is Frank Derrick, eighty-four, former manager of the RO (Rowe) Ranch. He has watched the Clarendon area's nutritious gramma, bluestem and rye grass give way to the invasion of cotton. In a 1991 interview Derrick explained, "If it hadn't been for the British and British money there wouldn't have been any large ranches."

Without European investment, dirt farmers would have borne the burden of settling the plains and mountain country with limited capital. Their ranches would have been small and inefficient. And—an unromantic footnote—cowboys might have worn overalls!

The second viewpoint carries modern economic overtones and was expressed by Byron Price, historian and head of the National Cowboy Hall of Fame in Oklahoma City. Price observed, "What the British did on the frontier was very similar to what the Japanese are doing in the United States today."

What the British did was fill the great plains with ranches so huge they sprawled across many counties. The XIT Ranch—whose stock was floated in the world financial capital of London—totaled three million acres. At that time it was the largest ranch enclosed by fence anywhere in the world.

Although the RO Ranch was never that large, Alfred Rowe was the quintessential British cattleman. He came in 1879—very English and already a worldly traveler with the itchy feet of a remittance man. But at twenty-six, when he arrived in the Panhandle, he already possessed practical agricultural training and had the ability to put aside his gentlemanly etiquette to sit comfortably on the ground around an open-range campfire, chatting with his cowboys.

The Panhandle, in fact, isn't the best place to look for remittance men. It harshly weeded out the half-hearted or uncommitted. Yet in superficial ways young Alfred Rowe *was* a remittance man. Certainly he was one of the most interesting of all British Texans, able to mix friendship and eccentricity in attractive proportions.

Alfred was reared in gentlemanly luxury and had early access to family wealth in Liverpool—although primogeniture decreed that he would never inherit the family estate. His elder brother, George, would be chief heir and Alfred and two other younger brothers, Bernard and Vincent, would be forced—or freed—to scour the world for adventure and opportunity. For a time the brothers joined the RO but finally tired of ranching and sold out.

Born February 24, 1853, Alfred had an early advantage. His birthplace actually was Lima, Peru, where his father temporarily located the family in pursuit of profits for Graham, Rowe & Company, the family's major shipping and trading firm. The foreign environment no doubt helped the Rowe sons get a feel for worldly business. In a few years, however, the family was back in Liverpool, where Alfred completed his education. He learned well.

When he arrived in Texas in 1879 to explore the Great Plains beef "miracle," he had a well-planned agenda and 500 pounds to finance the trip. His timing was perfect: By the late 1870s the heavy bullets of the buffalo hunters had largely cleared the rich grasslands of competition from the native bison.

But while many young Britons at this point would have been unsure of what to do next (except to write home for more money), Alfred Rowe had no such problems. With foresight (and a certificate from the Royal Agricultural College in Gloucester), he immediately took a job as a beginning cowboy on several ranches to learn the basics.

After choosing a ranch site near Old Clarendon (nicknamed Saints' Roost because its founders were fervently religious), Rowe in 1880 sent home for a family loan to buy the land. The total spent for land is unspecified, but according to his diary Rowe paid 11,452 dollars for 818 cattle (at 14 dollars per head); 760 dollars for twenty-six horses at 30 dollars each and some 200 dollars for a wagon and other equipment, including a 25-dollar revolver. With this modest outlay—and with cowboys working for 25 dollars a month—he soon repaid his family's loan although he continued to buy more land.

By 1900 he owned one hundred thousand acres and ran ten thousand head of cattle. By then he had moved the RO headquarters to the River Ranch described previously, a few miles from present-day Clarendon, which, in 1887, became a division point on the newly arrived Fort Worth & Denver City Railroad. Old Clarendon swallowed its saintly pride and joined the new town.

But if Alfred Rowe was too responsible to classify as a remittance man (although he used family money to get started) he had many quixotic characteristics of remittance men: an ironic quirk and the same restlessness of spirit that propelled the breed to the far corners of the globe. Three decades later he still hadn't decided whether to stay in Texas or go home.

How Britons like Rowe came to the high plains grasslands of Texas, New Mexico and Colorado—and by extension to Wyoming and other northern plains states—is a fascinating story of foolishness mixed with hardheaded investment principles. Alfred Rowe provided both.

He was described as totally honest, once telling a cattle buyer, "I haven't much to offer this year. My three-year-olds look like two-year-olds, my two-year-olds look like yearlings, and my one-year-olds look . . . like hell."

But he upgraded his stock with British breeds, including Durhams, and usually received top-of-the-market prices at Kansas City when he sold. He often was in a hurry, according to Fred Russell, ninety-four, an old-time cowboy who was interviewed in a Clarendon seniors' home in 1991.

"He never trotted his horse," said Russell. "It was always a walk or a run or a lope—never a trot."

Russell recalled that, as a small boy, he liked to climb the coal chutes in McLean, Texas, to watch RO cowboys load cattle on the train. He and other boys were noisy one day and Alfred Rowe, then in middle age, rode up at a gallop and shouted, "You damn kids keep quiet."

His riding style exasperated his cowboys. In Rowe's early years in Texas he would ride up to a roundup camp at a full gallop—"like a bloomin' Bengal Lancer," someone said. The commotion scattered the cattle, and his cowboys had to begin again the task of bunching the cattle for branding and castration.

He also had a habit of disappearing unexpectedly, only to reappear just as suddenly. He might send a postcard from London or Italy. One year he left in April and didn't return until Christmas. After another long absence he came in by train from New York and hired a driver to bring him to the ranch, apparently to settle in for a long stay. But in the morning, when the driver was preparing to leave, Alfred called out—"Wait!" Within a few minutes he had packed his bags again and left with the driver to return to England.

One summer evening he craved a cooling drink that required claret wine. He had a horse saddled and rode the fifteen miles into Clarendon, bought the wine and returned to share the drink at 2:00 A.M. with one of his cowboys. He could joke about himself. He once declared, "You know, it's a funny thing. When I'm in England, I'm Lord Rowe; when I'm in New York, I'm Mr. Rowe, but when I come out here I'm that S.O.B. Rowe." But on another occasion he reversed the theme to complain that he was a nobody in Britain—that his family were only wealthy commoners. Bones Hooks, a black cowboy employed by Rowe, once urged him to stay put in Texas and be a big man. Rowe explained why he didn't, "Well, I'm English. I suppose that is the only reason." So he continued his commuting across the Atlantic—a pattern that in 1912 would prove his undoing.

There were many other interesting Englishmen in the Panhandle. Almost pathetic was the Right Honorable Sir Cecil Archibald John Marjoribanks, sent out from London to manage the Rocking Chair Ranche, owned partly by his brother, the baron of Tweedmouth. The new manager ordered his cowboys to call him Sir Archibald. They responded by calling him Marshie, and would often charge at him full gallop, yelling like Indians and shooting around his feet.

Tweedmouth once visited the ranch and—though it pained him—democratically ate a meal with the cowboys while wearing his monocle. A cowboy asked, "Why does that old buzzard keep looking at me through his little peepglass?" The local Texas foreman, trying to be polite, responded, "His lordship is only admiring the way you handle beans with a knife."

When the other major owner, John Gordon, earl of Aberdeen, turned up at the Ranche the cowboys had more stories to tell. Lord Aberdeen was on his honeymoon and when he and Lady Aberdeen arrived, his lordship tried to unload their luggage—but sank to the ground exhausted, saying, "Oh, I cawn't. I cawn't. I shall have to lie on the grahss." His bride cheerfully unloaded the luggage and later helped prepare dinner while the manager's wife milked her cows.

Inattention to detail cost British investors dearly and the Rocking Chair was a good example. While Sir Archibald was drinking and chasing coyotes with his hounds, the firm's English foreman, John Drew, lined his own pockets with the cattle profits of the 150,000 acre ranch. It was only when neighboring ranchers joined to challenge Drew's depredations that a court ordered Drew and his ringleaders to leave the county forever or face the hangman.

The pantheon of wealthy Britons in the Panhandle centered around an American—a cowman any Western historian would rate tops—Charles Goodnight. Scores of books have been written about Goodnight. Not only was he a fine rancher; he cared about people. He loaned Alfred Rowe his foreman to help the young Englishman get his start. He helped launch the career of that superb ranch manager, the Scotsman Murdo Mackenzie.

Goodnight had the advantage of getting in on the ground floor. He drove his first herd of Texas longhorns to Indian reservations in the New Mexico territory in 1866 and marketed them to federal officials as food for Indian reservations. With the profits from the sale he began ranching on the Arkansas River near Pueblo, Colorado. It was in Colorado that he met John George Adair, a wealthy Irishman and his highborn American wife, Cornelia Wadsworth Ritchie, daughter of a Civil War general and widow of a colonel. Both died in the war. Cornelia's marriage to Adair was an odd union.

Known as Black Adair in Kildare, Ireland, this Scotch-Irish landlord's savage reputation preceded him to America. He had engaged in bitter struggles with his Irish tenants and finally evicted scores of them, burning their houses and forcing them to Australia or the workhouse—an action that paralleled Scotland's brutal clearings of small farms for sheep.

After powerful hatreds sank deep into local consciousness, Adair found travel diverting—and perhaps safer. It was in London that he met the attractive Cornelia. When the newlyweds settled down amidst the Wadsworth estates at Geneseo, New York, Cornelia's relatives disliked their fiery, black-bearded in-law.

He couldn't get along with either business associates or relatives and family pressure probably sent the couple west. They hunted bison in Nebraska, where Adair killed no game but accidentally put a bullet through the brain of the horse he was riding.

Charles Goodnight, Colorado and Texas cattleman, whose partnership with an Irish landowner became one of the most profitable of Western ranching ventures. (Photo courtesy of the Denver Public Library, Western History Department.)

Arriving in Denver, Adair opened a brokerage office and it was in this role—as an investor—that he met Goodnight. From this meeting came one of the greatest of all cattle empires. The Adairs had capital and Goodnight had ranching know-how. It was a partnership made in cow heaven. Adair's 1877 contract with Goodnight was comparable to investing in a business partnership with Henry Ford in 1915.

Goodnight was simply the best. He moved the partnership to the sprawling Palo Duro Canyon in the Panhandle. With its

John George Adair formed a partnership with Goodnight out of which came one of the largest cattle empires in the Southwest. Adair had the capital and Goodnight had the ranching know-how. (Photo courtesy of the Panhandle-Plains Historical Museum, Canyon, Texas.)

rock walls and brushy environment the spread required little fencing and gave the cattle protection from the elements. In the first five years he earned the partnership 512,000 dollars, a third of which was his. A second five-year partnership expanded the JA (for John Adair) to hundreds of thousands of acres; over the ten years the JA produced a 72 percent annual profit.

John Adair died in 1885, and when the second five-year contract expired, Goodnight divided the ranch with Mrs. Adair. He bought 160 sections for his own use, while Mrs. Adair kept the Palo Duro range. Both profited mightily. There is today a town named Goodnight east of Amarillo, and some of Mrs. Adair's land is still in the family (she had no children by Adair but had two by her first husband, Colonel Montgomery Ritchie of Boston).

In 1991, her grandson, an elderly Montie Ritchie, still headed the JA but devoted his leisure time to a delightfully secluded auxiliary ranch near Larkspur, Colorado. So the venture that started with Goodnight in the Colorado foothills near Pueblo still has sturdy roots in this same Front Range a century later.

The history of the JA in many ways is the history of western cattle. It symbolized Anglo-American joint effort. Suffering the disruptions of the Civil War, Americans were ready to forgive the old colonial hatreds of the British to gain the capital to develop their last frontier. The relationship with John Adair was a case in point. An unpleasant man from an alien way of life, he was tolerated because he had money.

The Adairs enjoyed life at the JA Ranch, which sprawled through several counties, but it was here that Adair learned that Texans weren't subservient Irish peasants. Montie Ritchie says Adair's "superior attitude didn't go too well," and that "trouble started the first day when he ordered a cowboy to, 'Saddle my horse, my man.' " Adair got an earful of Texas profanity and was lucky to escape physical assault. Ritchie tells the story with amusement, but when asked if he disliked Adair, he responds, "Did anyone like him?"

But didn't Adair change and show compassion in the JA's much-balleyhooed action in helping small squatters (illegal settlers) trade for land outside the JA's mammoth confines?

Montie Ritchie makes a quick response: "He didn't reform. He was dead when that happened." So give the credit for a humane act—almost the reverse of Adair's conduct in Ireland—to Goodnight and Mrs. Adair.

Adair's reactions typified the friction British gentry experienced when they collided with the frontier concept that a man who proved himself was the equal of anyone else, aristocracy included. Adair's snobbishness was pervasive, even among flat-broke remittance men. They were prisoners of an ancient class system that required them to defend its pecking order, no matter how outmoded. In their hearts they never left home.

Strip away Adair's powerful connections through his Wadsworth wife and his lucky partnership with Goodnight and—by American standards—he wasn't much of a cattleman. He was more the remittance man who issued his own checks.

The Anglo-American alliance struggled on in Texas and the West, often saved at the last minute by the British sense of fair-play and American pragmatism. The beneficial flood of capital continued as the British public absorbed a constant barrage of get-rich-quick stories about the West. Britain had supported Texas' battle for independence, so newspaper-reading Britons were familiar with Lone Star politics and geography. And now, late in the century, they were ready to invest in the can't-lose opportunities touted for the area's ranching.

If frontier excitement was the pull there also was a push. Because the Industrial Revolution's expansion was tapering off, British bankers were advising their clients to look overseas for interest rates better than the 2 or 3 percent paid in Britain. Even the middle-class depended on investment for basic income, so they eagerly bought shares in development companies. Wealthier investors came in person or sent a second son or nephew (hopefully competent) to the New World with the promise of a nest egg if he learned the ropes and found a good prospect.

Thus, of the sixteen hundred people counted in the Panhandle in the late 1870s, the vast majority were Anglo-Americans. By the mid-1880s the number was in the thousands, with Britons still ranking as the main foreign component. Britons loomed larger than life because they were adventurous and had money.

But give credit, too, to a large group of no-nonsense Scotsmen in green eyeshades in Edinburgh and Dundee. The Scottish bankers were ready when ranching opportunities opened up. They formed trusts to finance ranches from Oregon to South Texas. Their holdings spilled across state lines in Colorado, New Mexico, Texas, Wyoming and the Dakota Territory. Among their distinguished holdings was the great Matador Ranch, which was one of the best of all British ventures. Goodnight's protégé, Murdo Mackenzie, built the Matador to mammoth size in the 1890s. He managed so well that he survived the storms—real and economic—that sooner or later sank most of the big ranches. But he had good support from Scotland. One observer said, "The Boot Hills of the western American mortgage companies, numerous as they are, contain the bones of no major Scottish mortgage companies." The Matador averaged 15 percent annual earnings for thirty years and finally was sold in 1949 for 19 million dollars, thirty times the valuation placed on it before oil was found nearby.

Wherever British fancy pointed, Scottish moneylenders were close behind. Even Mrs. Adair and Goodnight financed several cattle purchases in Scotland. When the Scottish lenders discovered bookkeeping trouble at the great Swan Ranch in Wyoming, they sent a Scottish troubleshooter to count the cattle. He drew amused snickers from the cowboys when he tried to paint brands on the cattle to make a proper count. Rain washed off the brands. But Scottish financial experts kept the Swan going well into the twentieth century, until it finally went under.

Ironically, British investment was the key to construction of the Texas Statehouse. Needing a new capitol building in 1881, the Texas Constitutional Convention set aside three million acres of state land in the Panhandle as trade bait. A syndicate of Chicago businessmen took on the project, agreeing to build a three-million-dollar capitol in return for the land. This was the origin of the XIT, which ran 150,000 cattle over ten counties, and was so large that surveyors mapping the Texas–New Mexico line simply adopted the XIT's western fence line as the new state line for some one hundred miles. It covered ten counties. Texas lawmakers, opposed to foreign land ownership, found themselves sitting in the largest of all U.S. Statehouses thanks to British capital. Unable to find enough U.S. buyers, the syndicate had gone to London to sell their bonds.

Many other British-financed ranches fill Western history books: the Prairie Cattle Co., Ltd., with the earl of Airlie as chairman, sprawled across the Colorado line into New Mexico Territory and Texas; Wyoming's Anglo-American Cattle Company included a directorship for Sir John Rae Reid of London.

The advantage of these well-capitalized British ventures lay in size and efficiency. With the larger cattle herds, the unit cost of carrying an animal to marketable size dropped dramatically. Without British money, small American ranchers eventually would have homesteaded the territories, but only with small herds to fill the fifty-year gap between open prairies and the arrival of cotton and grain farming and intensive cattle feeding.

The advantages can be debated, but Alfred Rowe and his fellow Britons not only accelerated agricultural development, they also had capital to invest in the growing towns in the new territories. Their money had an electric quality; it charged the plains with a powerful sense of adventure and progress. Their worldly connections, good manners and well-tailored clothing gave local residents some idea of the world beyond.

Alfred Rowe was such a figure—a charming, keen-minded dabbler in the gaudy cattle bonanza. And in time he matured, surrendering some of his wanderlust. At forty-seven, he married Constance Kingsley, kin of a prominent English writer, Charles Kingsley. She bore him several children, and although Constance enjoyed Texas, her husband finally moved the family to Britain. But Alfred kept on commuting across the Atlantic to keep the ranch running smoothly.

It was with genuine sorrow that Clarendon received word by telegraph on April 15, 1912, that Alfred Rowe had died in the sinking of the *Titanic*. His cowboys missed him because he was one Britisher who could put aside his class consciousness at a chuckwagon cooking fire and enjoy simple cowboy talk. His courage was unchallenged. When the *Titanic* sank, Rowe refused to climb into a lifeboat because it was already overloaded. A strong swimmer, he stayed in the icy water and perished.

But a mystery died with him. In 1912, his friends in Clarendon said he had gone to England to discuss the future of the RO Ranch. He had taken along the familiar document-stuffed briefcase he always kept within reach. When the follow-up stories on the Titanic came in, Clarendon learned that Rowe's body was found on an iceberg, perhaps the one that sank the ship. Some stories say the briefcase was still clutched in his hand. But what was in it? Did it contain bank drafts to expand the ranch? Or might Rowe have gotten bored and decided to sell? Clarendon never found out and by 1918 the question was moot. His brothers completed the sale of the RO Ranch to an American, W. J. Lewis, who has held the ranch for seventy-five years.

As today's visitor ponders the old RO ranchhouse northeast of Clarendon, he or she realizes that—like its patrician builder—the graceful structure is a fitting memorial to the whole British era. From his fee land of nearly one hundred thousand acres Rowe controlled water courses and effectively ran cattle on some three hundred thousand acres, one of the best ranches in the Panhandle.

The RO brand has stayed with the ranch. Betty Boston, the wife of a recent owner of the RO, is fascinated by the history of the River Ranch and shows it proudly to visitors. Building on the British generations that went before, she and other ranch families have put down deep roots in the Panhandle.

✦
<hr />

A Nineteenth-Century
Old Boy Network

When British gentlemen and their ladies toured the American West they traveled in style and with good connections. Even young remittance men carried letters of introduction to influential people from whom they might seek advice, a job or help with an investment.

In 1832, William Drummond Stewart (later a Scottish baronet when his brother died) landed in St. Louis with excellent credentials. He immediately sought out the famous explorer, General William Clark, who had crossed the continent in 1805. As superintendent of Indian Affairs, Clark put Stewart in touch with the famous fur traders, Pierre Choteau, Jr., and General William Ashley, who helped Stewart join a fur trading party to the Indian country.

In 1855, when Lord St. George Gore, an Irish peer, came west to hunt, he traveled in comfort. He hired the preeminent mountain man, Jim Bridger, to supervise his lavish expedition, which included forty servants and nearly thirty wagons and other vehicles. The baronet killed all the major species of game, including three thousand buffalo and forty grizzly bears.

Influential Americans traveled well, too. In the 1870s, when the wealthy Irishman, John George Adair, arranged a Nebraska buffalo hunt for his wife, Cornelia, the party was given a U.S. Cavalry escort by the war hero and western army commander, Lieutenant General Philip H. Sheridan. Sheridan's reasons were personal. During the Civil War he had served under Cornelia's wealthy father, General James S. Wadsworth, killed in the Battle of the Wilderness. Safeguarding Wadsworth's daughter was Sheridan's way of showing respect for his old commander. Even after the Adairs became Texas ranchers, cavalry troops often stopped by to check on their safety.

The British insisted on good hotels. Arriving in St. Louis, Gore chose a suite of rooms at the five-story Planter's Hotel.

Well-appointed and properly Victorian, it served a jumping-off place for his western safari. The Windsor in Denver was a beacon on the western plains. Built by a Scottish investor, this large hotel offered excellent food and lodging for several decades. Europeans who traveled for their health knew by way of advertisements where the famous western spas were. Colorado Springs became known as Li'l Lunnon because of the hordes of well-dressed British visitors. And when Lillie Langtry, the beautiful and talented English actress, appeared on the stage in Cheyenne, she traveled in a private rail car supplied by American friends.

❖

CHAPTER 8

"Tallyho" in Kansas

By the 1880s there were remittance men all over the globe, embarrassing Britannia with their follies and reminding her that hat all was not well with her social and class system.

—*Richard A. Bartlett, historian*

By late Victorian times, Britain's class structure had gone to seed. The fearless military commanders had retired and were mentioned mostly in the obituary columns of the *London Times*. Their callow heirs searched not for conquest but soft pleasures and adventure. There is no better time or place to witness the contrast than nineteenth-century Kansas.

With Britain prosperous and mostly at peace, these young sons of the wealthy sought a solution to their boredom in migration, and some of them landed in Kansas. They settled near Hays, Kansas, probably not far from where bloody Spanish conquerors planted a European flag three centuries earlier—but they didn't grasp that hardy symbolism, either.

What the young Britons were interested in was fun. They also fully intended to re-create their class system along the creek bottoms and on the prairies of the West. Theirs was an incredible combination of arrogance and naïveté that produced endless heartbreak and pathos. It also produced hilarity.

Imagine you are in an arid section of the Great American Desert near Hays and its companion military post, Fort Hays. The time is the 1870s.

You are a witness as a handful of young British heirs—some single, some married—follow the leadership of a rich London merchant named George Grant in building a colony loyally named Victoria. But they are dispirited: There are no lakes for the water sports they enjoyed in England.

Fortune smiles. Henry Edward and Sidney Fenwick Smithe, playboy brothers from Britain, are present—and equal to the challenge. Their father had launched them in the direction of Kansas with the promise of monthly remittances. But now the brothers have something better than remittances. While they were en route to Kansas, their father died, and so they are in the chips. They not only have shared in his 18,000-pound estate; they also have sold everything else their father owned, including his London wine business and his vineyards in Spain. They have perhaps 1 million dollars to spend—a huge amount in those days.

And spend it they do. The problem of water sports is quickly solved. Henry Smithe, the elder brother, contracts to have a dam

A handful of young British heirs followed George Grant to Victoria, Kansas, to establish a British community. But the colony dwindled when the pursuit of fun rather than industry left farmland covered with weeds.

built at Victoria. It backs water eight miles up Big Creek, past Hays and nearly to old Fort Hays. Fifteen feet deep, it handles with ease Henry's next purchase—a sixteen-foot steam-powered launch shipped out from St. Louis. Henry then builds a wharf near the three-thousand-acre farm he had purchased on arrival.

But the launching of the *Jolly West* on March 23, 1878, is a disaster mercifully witnessed by only a handful of invitees. These successors to Drake and Nelson forgot the ballast. The little vessel—fitted with polished brass and mahogany deckwork—slides down the skids, rides majestically for a few seconds and then slowly turns turtle, nearly drowning a Frenchman who is scarcely able to dog paddle.

Soon righted, however, the *Jolly West*—now with sandbags in the hold—chugs gloriously up to Fort Hays, where soldiers and Indians give it a noisy welcome.

The sight of black smoke pouring from a steamboat navigating the prairies of Kansas must have been a shock to westbound pioneers traveling the dusty trails in their ox-drawn wagons.

But such goings-on soon became the norm, especially when the Smithes were involved. Their arrival in Hays was, in itself, an incident that made jaws drop. They got off the train dressed for Bond Street, followed by a butler and his wife and the other servants. The 500,000-dollar mansion they erected near Victoria was the talk of Ellis County. Its rooms were huge, trimmed with hardwood and served by a stately walnut stairway leading to the second story. The large dining room was equipped with a bar, and around the house was a lush, five-acre garden that looked as if it had been replanted directly from Kent.

To neighboring farmers living in sod houses, the surprise must have been almost as great as the steamboat.

The Smithes weren't through shocking their neighbors, however. Their parties were splendid; the Hunt Club held its first meeting at their house, with twenty caterers arriving by rail from Denver to serve "a light repast." And when Henry married an English actress named Lucy Buckstone, she matched his eccentricities. She delighted in taking her bath when it rained—on a balcony fully visible to the farmhands tilling Henry's fields. There is no record that they complained.

How this British colony—its decadence built in—came to life on the Kansas plains was due to the visionary and energetic George Grant, whose grave is one of the few left in Victoria.

Grant was a poor Scots boy who migrated to London. Doing well as a silk merchant, he had a lucky hunch in 1861. Reading a newspaper report that Queen Victoria's beloved consort, Prince Albert, was seriously ill, Grant realized that if the Prince died all England would be draped in black for mourning. So he bought all the black crepe he could find and managed to corner the market sufficiently so that when the Prince succumbed a few days later Grant made the British equivalent of 1 million dollars. With this money he bought seventy-two thousand acres of land near Hays from the Kansas Pacific Railroad. Grant then resold the land to colonists.

A few colonists actually were experienced British farmers and their descendants still run farms and businesses today. But far too many did not come for the long pull and, after a few years, cleared out. Natural hazards admittedly were difficult—drought, prairie fire, grasshoppers and blizzards.

But there were too many remittance men like the Smithes who, despite plunging into debt, still kept up socially. After all, they were British and upper class. How hard they worked at socializing is shown by the Victoria Hunt Club. Organized March 15, 1877, it elected traditional officers, including a Master of the Hunt. When their women joined the hunt it was in red coats, derbies, riding skirts and boots, but they rode side-saddle.

In scheduling their grand Hunt Ball, members jumped the gun on the weather and wound up in a late March blizzard. But they persevered by driving sleighs to their rented hall in Hays. Women wore formal dresses; a few male escorts wore red swallow-tailed hunting garb.

The *Hays City Star* society editor described the ladies as "beautifully dressed" and reported that the dances included quadrilles, waltzes, reels, Schottisches and polkas. Some of the British women remained storm-bound in Victoria, but American ladies from Hays turned out in enough strength to provide each man a partner. It was a beautiful and cultured word picture and a rare one for the West. Few places between Denver and Kansas City would see anything like the high society of Victoria for many years.

But the excitement of living on the exotic frontier began to lag and boredom inevitably followed. Grant kept the faith by borrowing money to encourage settlers to stay and to keep new ones coming. But it was a losing effort and the railroad foreclosed on part of Grant's land in the mid-1870s. He died on April 28, 1878, and gradually the colony dwindled. In economic terms, Victoria was its own worst enemy. Grant's recruitment policies aimed at bringing moneyed young Britons to Victoria. They had the money to pay his prices for the land. But if, like the Smithes, they had the money they also were gentlemen. That meant they wanted to have fun playing cricket and polo and pursuing wild antelope and jackrabbits across the prairie with packs of greyhounds. Their farmland grew weeds.

A remarkable irony developed. While Victoria dwindled, a strong colony of Volga Germans was settling in beside Victoria—in fact, the German settlement must soon have adopted the name Victoria because little remained of the British colony ten years after Grant's death. Grant's tomb credits him with importing the first Aberdeen Angus cattle to the American West. But the Volga Germans brought something just as important—the ability to grow dryland wheat and help make Kansas the nation's breadbasket. These newcomers were Germans whose ancestors had moved to the Volga area while the German princess Catherine the Great ruled Russia. They fled when her pledge of exemption from conscription into the Russian army expired. Good farmers, they settled throughout the Great Plains. Victoria today is *their* colony. About all the visitor can see of original Victoria today is the well-tended graveyard where Grant and a few other Britons are buried.

Long before motorists arrive on Interstate 70, they can see far in the distance the great Catholic church the Germans built—the Cathedral of the Plains—at Victoria. The Episcopal Church is long gone; Presbyterians took its stones for their church at Hays.

Victoria is one of the more spectacular failures, but the scenario was being repeated in many other places, including several in Kansas. The territory was an early battleground over slavery, resulting in passage by Congress of the Kansas-Nebraska Act in 1854 and subsequent statehood for Kansas in 1861, earlier than other western areas. As a state, Kansas soon had the legal mechanisms for land purchase and development. Other early British colonies included Wakefield, in north central Kansas in 1869, and Runnymede, founded in 1886 near Harper, only a few miles north of today's Oklahoma.

Wakefield persevered because its settlers were middle class British farmers, but Runnymede was infected, like a worm in the bud, by the class system that sank Victoria. Its promoters worked the British upper classes for money to establish their own squiredoms. For 500 dollars a young British gentleman could build up a country estate in the new world, providing himself both wealth from livestock and leisure time to pursue sports and social companionship in his local clubs, or so the promoters said.

The organizer of Runnymede—named for the place in England where in 1215 a reluctant King John gave Englishmen their equivalent of the U.S. Bill of Rights—was Francis J.S. (Ned) Turnly. Arriving in the mid-1880s from County Antrim in Ireland, he had the money and vision to make Runnymede work—for awhile.

At its peak Runnymede had some fifty-seven families, nearly all recruited in Britain by Turnly. Many were remittance men, and Captain Charles Seton, a member of the colony, blamed them and general naïveté when Runnymede collapsed in a few years, calling Runnymede:

> A combination of British inexperience, credulity, some money, considerable cockneyism, withal a jolly lot of men and women transported to the bold Kansas prairie, where the immigrants expected to grow rich in a day and a night and then return to England where they would live ever afterwards on champagne and venison. Two years wore off the varnish, broke the bank, and turned out the lights. But Rome howled in the interim.

While it lasted, Runnymede had English manor houses, tennis courts, polo grounds, a steeplechase course and other frivolities that baffled local residents. They dressed both as British gentlemen and as heavily armed frontiersmen. One colonist reportedly made himself look so dangerous he scared himself.

All of this may have been related to the heavy drinking that went on in Runnymede. Parents in England, sending off their remittances, hoped that Kansas' early dedication to prohibition would curb their sons' alcoholism but whiskey was easily ordered and shipped from Chicago. So the remittances were withdrawn, the colonists moved elsewhere (or back to Britain) and Runnymede's attractive buildings were cannibalized by neighboring towns; the imposing hotel, the Runnymede Arms, was carried off to Alva, Oklahoma.

But remittance men shouldn't bear all the burden of failure for the British-American colonies. Successful promoters sold a good deal more than cheap land. To young male customers they played the Buffalo Bill theme: "Ah, you must see the mountains, hunt wild game and mingle with the exotic peoples of the New World!" The tactic worked well with those who had only read the inflated adventure stories of the New World. On a slightly broader and restrained level, the typical sales pitch promised plenty of time for socializing, literary clubs, cricket, polo and steeplechasing—things cultured Britons enjoyed while servants did the work of cultivation and caring for the livestock.

Britain also was rich ground for tillers of the reformist soil. Ever since colonial days the eastern North American seaboard had been the target of groups seeking religious freedom and the creation of societies anchored in dogma and idealistic faiths. The Pilgrims and Quakers were only the beginning.

One of the most interesting promoters to emerge in the latter part of the century was an idealistic novelist, Thomas Hughes, who launched perhaps the strangest colony of all at Rugby, Tennessee in 1879. Hughes was rich and famous as author of the novel *Tom Brown's School Days*, which was based on life at the honored British public school, Rugby. Rugby glorified sport and instilled in upper class boys the ideals of gentlemanly conduct, along with courage and a sense of fair play. Rugby taught the classics, Latin and Greek, and prepared its pupils to move on to Cambridge or Oxford.

While Hughes' writing fully accepted the British class system, in his heart he was a reformer and he saw the problems created when upper class families sent their sons out like loose cannons aimed at the frontier. So with his ample publishing royalties and the support of wealthy sympathizers, he chose for his colony a site in the Cumberland Hills of eastern Tennessee. His English Emigration Association bought seventy-five thousand acres in a region deemed ideal for small farms of forty to fifty acres supplying fruit to a cannery. Migrants were expected to maintain a high moral standard, shunning liquor and the worst abuses of commercialism.

But when idealism is applied to practicalities it often falls hardest. After Hughes built sixty-five dwellings, a church and other public buildings the colony began a downhill slide. Temperance was a problem and the press soon poked fun at Rugby, claiming that many a settler entered the woods and, happening upon a moonshiner, would say, "Beg pardon, sir, I would like to loan you a dollar." Overcome by the Briton's generous act, the grateful moonshiner would reach into a hollow tree and hand over a sociable bottle of white lightning as security for the loan.

Rugby probably had no chance from the beginning, but an outbreak of typhoid, the failure of the canning plant and outmigration soon doomed the little community. And, let's face it, those jolly expatriates, the remittance men, also were present, loafing. A British woman who visited Rugby and found stores closed, houses empty and many colonists devoted to billiards and hunting, observed that many were young wastrels: "Some young men of that kind whose return would be a terror to their families remain there, living on doles from home, supplemented by what they get by sport.... " This is a classic definition of a remittance man: waiting for the check from home and soliciting funds from fellow Britons for cricket and other competitive sports.

So Rugby closed fewer than five years after it began, with only the Episcopal church still standing. And nowhere was there more sneering at Rugby's failure than in Le Mars, Iowa, where a more successful colony had been planted in the same year as Rugby by a clever British businessman, William B. Close, who with his brother, Fred, founded Close Brothers Ltd.

The Closes were everything Hughes wasn't. William Close inherited wealth but he worked hard. He was competitive and had captained the Cambridge rowing team. But more importantly he had escaped gentrification. This was because he was the fifth of eight children of an international banker who actually lived on his yacht in the Mediterranean and Adriatic, with a home base at Antibes, France. Here there was less focus on primogeniture in matters of inheritance. The four Close sons, of whom William was second oldest, were given equal educational opportunity and shared the family wealth after their father died in 1856. (Also, their mother was independently wealthy). Unlike other young Britons, William took seriously his father's advice: "Labour and industry are absolute requisites to independence and happiness."

Despite their distance from Britain, the Close family had important British cousins and friends in the aristocracy. These connections were to prove vital when William, finished with Cambridge, became a developer of Iowa farmland.

How this came about was the result of a faulty slide beneath William's seat in the Cambridge shell. The slide didn't work properly and, as he rowed, William suffered a back strain that sidelined him during a training session at Cape May, New Jersey. Reduced to circulating with the resort crowd, William met a wealthy land developer, Daniel Paullin, from Quincy, Illinois. They became friends. From Paullin, Close learned that there was a great deal of fertile land in northwestern Iowa, still undivided and unsold because it was in the form of railroad grants. (In time, William Close married Paullin's attractive daughter, Mary.)

Joined by his younger brother, Fred, in 1877, William first spent time at Denison in western Iowa and then made an offer of 2.40 dollars an acre on fourteen thousand acres in the Le Mars area in northwest Iowa. It was accepted and it was a steal. After subdivision and erection of buildings for resale in farm-sized plots, Close Brothers Ltd. ultimately made millions of dollars. But it all started with effective promotion. Some five hundred British colonists (and the successors who came to buy them out when the first settlers tired of Le Mars) couldn't resist the call of cheap land, not only because it was mildly rolling and good for growing grain but also because its timbered river courses made it ideal for fox hunting.

Close Brothers Ltd. actually was a Le Mars and Chicago firm but it maintained a branch office in London to sell farms to

British buyers. So brisk was travel between London and Le Mars that British steamship lines briefly listed Le Mars above New York City on their timetable postings of arrivals and departures.

Any wintertime resident of Iowa knows what a shock Le Mars must have been to the hopefuls arriving from Britain. Accustomed to an oceanic climate where warming air masses regularly relieve the cold spells and limit snowfall, they must have reeled in the face of the howling blizzards that regularly hit Iowa.

But the underlying fact was that climate was of small discomfort as long as the British colonist could maintain social position. Suffering from the cold was quite all right as long as one maintained dignity—and farming, strangely, was a permissible way to keep face. Of course, one should be a gentleman farmer with hired hands to do the work while the master joined other gentlemen to pursue foxes across the Iowa prairie.

As historian Curtis Harnack observed, "Europeans have emigrated (sic) to the United States for a variety of reasons, but rarely has it been 'the thing to do' to preserve social status." Yet a large colony of wealthy British gentlemen flourished at Le Mars, attended by servants and farm workers, and spent from 500 to 600 dollars a month for general living expenses.

Many of these families had noble blood. Contrast this to German immigration in the same century. Statistics show that more than 90 percent of all German migrants to the United States came from low economic levels. If they had worked in German factories it was as heavy laborers. If farmers, their work had been in heavy tilling, not in livestock or as orchard specialists. Such people came with virtually nothing; necessity told them they were in America to stay.

But the British had many options. They were in Iowa on a tryout. The family estates at home were still wealthy, but Britain was undergoing a farm depression, triggered by cheap foodstuffs from abroad. So surplus sons whose status wouldn't permit them to take an industrial job at home sought farming in far-off places as a suitable—and possibly temporary—alternative. Because of their education, some ultimately found administrative jobs in the United States or Canada. A few kept wandering, planting tea in Southeast Asia or running sheep stations in Australia.

But while the British era lasted in northwest Iowa—and it persevered well into the new century—it was a sight to behold. Sir Horace Plunkett, who operated a ranch in Wyoming, stopped at Le Mars for a visit and observed Lord Hobart, heir to the earldom of Buckinghamshire, barefoot and following the plow. "True, I never saw anyone more like a ploughboy and less like an earl," said Plunkett, "but the blood is there … ."

Close Brothers at various times owned about four hundred thousand acres of land in Iowa, Minnesota and elsewhere as they built up their wealth. But even the Close brothers tired of farming. William brought another brother, James, into the firm after Fred was killed in a fall during a polo match at Sioux City, Iowa. Close Brothers went to Alaska and built the Skagway to Yukon railroad at tremendous cost in men (thirty-five deaths) and money (a total investment of 7 million dollars). Yet their railroad turned a profit.

Only a handful of descendants remain in Le Mars, but the Pantry Cafe is still full of customers and bustle. It was here the city's last remittance man, George Hotham, Jr., went every morning for breakfast for many years. Like his father before him he hadn't worked a day in his life and relied on family money—some of it invested in Le Mars property—for his support. Examine Burke's Peerage and you'll find that one of the Hothams was an admiral in the English fleet in the Napoleonic wars; later Hothams served the Empire in far-off colonial engagements. It was a powerful family, able to send George Hotham, Sr., 30 dollars a day in remittances at the turn of the last century. A tidy sum.

Thus went the course of British settlements in Kansas and other places from Texas to Canada. Their influence is invisibly embedded in U.S. society. One sees few of their structures today, although influences are everywhere in culture, language, custom and law. Only a few remittance men put down roots.

At Le Mars, Iowa, for example, some of their buildings exist, in remodeled form, but the pubs where the remittance men drank—the House of Lords, the House of Commons and the Windsor—are gone.

Le Mars is a pleasant community with a college that has been turned over, in part, to young students from Japan, some of whom are finding life in a foreign place most difficult, just as the English did a century ago.

When George Hotham, Jr., died at Le Mars in the 1980s (his father had died in 1948), he went to his grave proud of his English ancestry but proud, too, that his mother had been a German girl descended from the poor immigrants who took over the Iowa land from the British. So the Hothams, who roved the world as fighting men, here at least made a union with the German settlers whose bond with the land was permanent.

But it is still remarkable that Britain, with its undemocratic class system, was able to send its sons so far abroad—to adventure, buy land and leave their mark on far corners of the world. It is hard to comprehend wealth so entrenched that families could provide their sons with so many millions in remittances.

The visionary promoters of these colonies had a flawed dream but their failure often lay in their selection of their own kind—colonists of a gentlemanly class who migrated on a whim and in their hearts didn't plan to stay. When the fun was over they went home.

Yet it is hard to say the colonies failed. They flooded libraries with their books and magazines. They held grand swirling balls that must have enchanted little American boys and girls fortunate enough to peer through the ballroom windows. How much do latter-day American socialites in Kansas City and Denver owe to the roving gentlemen and ladies from Britain? How much of our architecture came from British blueprints?

But what of the Smithe family at Victoria? Their story is tragic. Forced into bankruptcy by his profligate spending, Henry loaded Lucy and their worldly goods into a wagon, said goodbye to their beautiful mansion and migrated first to Pueblo, Colorado, and then to Denver. To make ends meet Lucy returned to the stage, with only partial success. They returned to Britain where, according to reports, Henry was imprisoned for trying to kill Lucy so that he could marry another woman.

✤
_____

A Love Letter from Kentucky

February 14, 1843

Clara Thompson
with Sir William Gossett
29 A. Pall Mall, London

My Dear Clara,

    With the greatest pleasure I take up my pen to address you as my dearest friend I have on Earth. It is now about eight weeks since I wrote to you and not having a letter from you all that time I begin to think it must have been lost or else you must be weighing something great in your mind which is the cause of such delay. I sometimes think you must be waiting the consent of your friends on your coming to America. My only hope is that you will come to me and join me in this happy land of Universal Suffrage. As for the consent of your parents I have no expectation of your getting [it] for your coming to America will bring their grey hairs down with sorrow to the grave. But if I had the stupid good luck to have staid [sic] in England as a poor, degraded lickspital under some lordling Aristocrat then you would have had their consent most cheerfully to your coming ...to be made my wife by some moral blackguard of a Parson. ... The case would be altered as surely as the Atlantic is between us. My dear Clara! If I could only impress on your mind what I feel in mine how unhappy you would be until you quitted the shores of England. ... But this must be the last time I can ask you to come to me and I will leave for you to decide.

    I know you may think the undertaking too great for a lone female to take in hand. Clara dear, I know such is almost the case but the necessity is to be looked to before such fears take hold of you. There are hundreds of single females coming to

America every year ... some most probably you will say are the outcasts of society and wanderers from virtue ... some are, I must own but some are as virtuous lovely women as ever crossed the Ocean. ...

I wish I could speak to you instead of writing. I remain yours till death stills living and loving my Clara.

A. Mattison
Hopkinsville, KY

According to Charlotte Erickson, author of *Invisible Immigrants*, Andrew Mattison finally settled in Paducah, Kentucky, in 1850 and became a landowner. She says his letter probably was never answered because Mattison had left England knowing he could never marry Clara, whose social standing was higher than his own.

❖

CHAPTER 9

Hot-Rodding on Horseback

It was early 1887. Below the distant ramparts of Colorado's Front Range lay forty miles of snowy wasteland, white against the distant blue peaks. The scene was deceptively calm after a great brute of a storm that had raged for days over the plains country. Giant snowdrifts obscured much of the prairie but blue sky overhead and a warming western wind signaled the storm's departure.

The weather change was a relief for Lyulph Gilchrist Stanley Ogilvy, second son of a Scottish earl. Thanks to his family's money, the young man for five years had owned a three-thousand-acre ranch on Crow Creek near the frontier community of Greeley. Although his ranch boasted better grass than other properties and stored some hay for winter, Ogilvy's cattle still suffered some storm losses. Blizzards had pummeled the entire Great Plains region since November 4, and now, with the onset of snow-eating chinooks coming off the peaks, Ogilvy decided to assess the damage.

As he prepared to ride across the range he puzzled over something different and vaguely ominous that had been added to the distant landscape. Along his seven-mile drift fence that stretched southward to the Union Pacific Railroad line and South

Platte River, which ran parallel to each other, lay a long dark smudge that shouldn't be there. The more he tried to squint through the shimmering snow, the more mysterious the smudge became. Taking along several of his cowboys, Ogilvy rode out for a look.

They skirted huge drifts until they reached a vantage point where it all became clear: The dark smudges and white hummocks in the snow were dead cattle—seven miles of dead cattle

Lyulph Ogilvy (center with chest strap), son of the earl of Airlie, cut a wide swath through Colorado's ranching and journalistic scene. His father arranged the purchase of a Colorado ranch for Lyulph but while the son was a good stockman, he lost a great deal of family money through land and irrigation schemes. Flat broke in 1909 he became a farm writer for The Denver Post. *He's shown in the Boer War. (Photo from the collection of Jack Ogilvy.)*

piled against Ogilvy's drift fence, victims of one of the worst storms in decades, an event so devastating it would alter the whole course of Western development in the United States.

Even to a wealthy young Scotsman who had adventured over much of the United States and, before that, Europe, the scene that lay before him was mind-wrenching. As he rode along the fence he calculated that, with only a few jumps between clumps of frozen flesh, a man could walk those seven miles on the bony carcasses of hundreds of dead cattle without ever stepping on the ground. It was a story Lyulph Ogilvy would tell for the rest of his life; a century later his son, Jack Ogilvy, a retired English professor, would still relate it with a shudder. So, too, would generations of other ranch families all the way from Alberta, Canada, to the Texas Panhandle.

As Ogilvy and his cowboys worked down to the end of the fence in the brush and trees flanking the South Platte River, the scene became even more heart-breaking and graphic. The starving animals had desperately gnawed off stumps of cottonwood saplings, eating down to the thickness of a man's wrist. The lower branches of the larger trees hung like rags where they had been chewed.

Hunger was the basic cause of the disaster. But as the animals piled against the fence, moving with their backs to the blizzard, it was suffocation through crowding, with water freezing and clogging their nostrils, that caused their deaths. Perhaps a million cattle died that winter.

Some of the cattle carried Ogilvy's own Half-Diamond-L brand but most of them were from elsewhere. Some brands were from his own county of Weld, but many were from farther north—Wyoming and even Montana. With scarcely a fence between Colorado and the North Pole, the cattle had drifted south, wandering aimlessly, relentlessly, before the storms. Had some of them walked from Montana? Possibly, because the cattle had started moving south the previous year when drought, following heavy snow during the winter of 1885–86, compounded the overgrazing problem.

Desperate owners the previous fall had begun moving animals south and east in search of better range. They offered shares in their herds to any landowner willing to try to winter them. It was a losing gamble. Ranchers hugged their wood-burning stoves, unable to get outside, and the cattle herds scattered like leaves across the land, looking for forage that did not exist or was buried beneath crusted snow.

Had Congress investigated, it would have discovered one of the greatest scandals in the settlement of the West—the misuse of the land by get-rich-quick cattle investors, most of them Americans but also a disproportionately large share of wealthy Britons in search of easy money. With their own British investments paying no more than 2 or 3 percent, they sent their capital to the United States where returns were above 5 percent.

It was a sure thing—or so the Britons believed. U.S. cattle profits were simple mathematics. You bought a herd, turned it loose on the free western range, paid your managers about 70 cents a year per animal for maintenance and watched your investment skyrocket. After you paid only 15 to 20 dollars for a young steer, he would triple in weight on grass over a few years. Steers were commonly kept about five years, when, weighing one thousand pounds, they could bring 40 dollars in grass-fat condition. Adding to the profit were the calves born each year.

The investors, of course, didn't reckon with thieving Americans. On the range were the rustlers, ready with their running irons, and at the ranch house were the managers notorious for their over- and under-counts of cattle being bought and sold. It was a rare investor who knew anything about cattle except what he read in glowing annual reports, now suddenly subdued, issued by the hastily formed companies that had sold him the shares.

The reports were evasive because the tragedy of 1986–87 was slow in coming to light. The enormity of the losses was hard to grasp, for one thing.

But ranch managers also tried to hide the reality by sending in vague accounts that avoided the word "starvation" but spoke—as if it were an act of God—of an ailment called hollow gut. Pride or self-preservation balked at using the word "overgrazing."

Independent ranchers like Lyulph Ogilvy were angry. The storm validated Ogilvy's earlier decision to build an irrigation ditch from the Cache la Poudre River near Greeley to provide water to the semiarid ranch to irrigate hay and grain for his cattle. But he couldn't ignore the folly going on around him. He spoke bitterly of the cattle barons, including fellow Britons, calling them "pigs who overgrazed the land for a few years' profit."

There was mental anguish, too. Sensitive ranchers would never be free of the nightmare of waking to the sound of clicking horns as their starving herds walked endlessly around the ranch house looking for food. The pioneer Montana rancher Granville Stuart wrote in his memoirs, "I never again wanted to own an animal I could not feed and shelter."

Although it struck less widely, the next winter was, in human terms, worse. Mother Nature found a new way to twist the knife in the bodies and minds of settlers ignorant of the Great Plains and its climate. She delivered a terrible blow to their children.

It was warm, almost balmy, on the morning of January 12, 1888, encouraging people to wear light clothing. But between 3:00 and 4:00 P.M., one of the most terrible blizzards in history struck. Scores of rural children froze to death between the school house and home. They became hopelessly lost in the whiteout, sometimes perishing with their hands linked to each other and to their heroic teachers. It would forever be known in the Dakotas, Nebraska and Kansas as The Schoolchildren's Storm.

The message was clear: A rancher had to do something besides simply buying the water holes—like Ogilvy's Crow Creek—and then letting one's cattle graze the public lands. Every year was a gamble that the number of dead cattle would be acceptably low, permitting a profit. Ranchers now realized the gamble was too great. They would have to provide winter fodder to survive. Over the next few years implement makers shipped thousands of horse-drawn mowers to the West as ranchers cut and stacked irrigated hay to feed their stock through the winters.

It was into this world of deadly hidden hazards—a mountain and plains country whose extremes of beauty and wasteland balanced each other—that young Lyulph Ogilvy had migrated some five years earlier. He visited several Western states in 1881 with his father, the eighth earl of Airlie, who had lent his distinguished name to a Scottish trust formed at Dundee to invest in the manifold economic opportunities of western America. The trust survived but tragedy stalked the earl.

The earl's full name was David Graham Drummond Ogilvy. He was descended from one of Scotland's most prestigious families. They had fought the English and their own turf battles for a thousand years. It was only during David Graham's father's time that the earlship had been restored after a sixty-five-year withdrawal as punishment for the Ogilvys' support of Bonnie Prince Charlie's rebellion in 1745.

Now in 1881 the eighth earl was visiting the West on behalf of Scottish investors in the Alliance Trust of Dundee. What he wasn't advertising was that, although he might be the latest in a line of fierce warriors, his personal weakness was gambling. To recoup his fortunes he had lent his name to the trust that invested in farming schemes in Oregon and Washington territories and ranched in several other western states. It held stock in the famous Matador Ranch in Texas. The trust did well and survives to this day. But the 1881 trip was to end in tragedy.

Officially, the earl was on a trip of inspection. But he had visited the United States several times before and he now wanted his son, Lyulph, and his daughter, Maud, to see the fascinating new land of opportunity. Lyulph had left Eton after five forms— just short of qualifying for Oxford or Cambridge. But because of primogeniture, Lyulph's older brother, David Graham Stanley Ogilvy would inherit all the Airlie holdings of one hundred thousand acres in Scotland, including two big castles. There would thus be no future for Lyulph in Scotland. So the earl bought the Crow Creek Ranch near Greeley in 1881, apparently intending to make Lyulph an American rancher.

Using the famous Windsor Hotel in Denver (built with British money) as headquarters, the Ogilvys toured the West to inspect properties for a report to stockholders back home. The tragedy struck during a visit to New Mexico. The earl came down with an infection later diagnosed as typhoid. The three hurried back to the Windsor. It was there, at 11:00 A.M. on September 25, 1881, that the earl died.

The two grief-stricken young people brought their father's body back to Scotland amidst general shock. The earl was only fifty-five; the *London Times* mourned the loss of his agricultural expertise in Parliament. But after the burial Lyulph Ogilvy hurried back to Colorado to claim the Colorado ranch. During next two decades he would receive a total of some 300,000 dollars of family money to buy and run ranch property in Colorado. The money, some loans and some remittances of trust funds, came to Colorado, in the words of his son Jack, "from time to time."

Lyulph—pronounced "Lilf," meaning "wolf" in Gaelic—was born June 5, 1861, in London, where his family kept a town house. But his real home was Cortachy Castle north of Dundee, near the small village of Kirrimuir, which was the birthplace of a more famous Ogilvy kinsman, Sir James Barrie of *Peter Pan* fame. Dundee is on the Firth of Tay and draws on the hinterlands of northeastern Scotland for its international trade, which made it Scotland's third largest city.

Lyulph's older brother, David, was clumsy and slow, but he was a credible ninth earl of Airlie, attending Eton and Oxford and becoming a professional army officer. Young Lyulph's path as a second son was more turbulent. After Eton, he gained a lieutenancy in the Lanark Militia, a second-rate military organization. But mainly, as a younger son with reduced prospects, he indulged in his favorite sport, fox hunting.

Some of the most famous people of the day, writers like Thomas Carlyle, William Thackeray and John Ruskin and politicians like William Gladstone and Benjamin Disraeli, were frequent visitors to the Ogilvy residences. The Countess Blanche Ogilvy, who outlived her husband by forty years, hoped the social mingling would infuse her sons with intellectual ambitions, but it didn't work. David, the new earl, was content to be a plodding army man and Lyulph was set on a life of action.

Within a year of his father's death the tall young Scot was in Colorado to stay, delighted to trade a world of privilege for adventure in the wild American West as a cattle rancher. Was there any anguish in seeing his elder brother "scoop the lot" in terms of inheritance? Elvon Howe, a Denver journalist who worked with Lyulph at the *Post*, argued that, "Like most second sons he was land-hungry." If the fruit was forbidden, he wanted it.

So Crow Creek Ranch spelled both escape and opportunity to Lyulph. But he was also barely twenty and an undisciplined, if a well-educated Etonian. His arrival in Greeley, therefore, signaled not only a lively, progressive ranching presence but a level of sustained hell-raising the West still talks about.

"When you live in a country, live *with* it," said young Lyulph, who suited his actions to the word by involving himself in numerous land deals, digging irrigation ditches and breaking hundreds of wild broncos, all with a flat English-style saddle. He also bred his own greyhounds to chase wolves, jackrabbits and other swift creatures of the plains.

His equestrian exploits are legendary. One vicious bronco seemed so intractable that Ogilvy vowed to ride him every day for a month and either tame him or sell him. By mid-month Ogilvy was a mass of contusions but on the twenty-seventh day the horse gave up and meekly consented to being a cow horse. But the beast still was a superb bucking horse and was sold, eventually to join Buffalo Bill's rodeo string for a grand tour of Europe.

Months later cowboys were discussing this famous rodeo horse in a Denver saloon, motivated by the news that the horse had finally been shot to death in Liverpool after breaking his leg sunfishing a rider to the ground. Ogilvy overheard the superlatives and quietly said, "I know the horse. I rode him around my place for six weeks—with a flat saddle."

Nobody challenged Ogilvy. They knew his reputation.

With a spirited horse or team he was the equivalent of a latter-day hot rodder. Meeting a train in Greeley, he once gave a ride to a visiting Britisher who expressed doubt that Ogilvy's "small" western horses could run, setting in motion a dramatic series of events.

"Let's see if they can," cried Ogilvy as he threw the reins on the horses' backs and laid on the whip. The hysterical runaways came to a halt two miles away, with little besides splinters left of the buggy. The Britisher, cradling a broken arm, said nothing more about Ogilvy's horses.

Another time, in Cheyenne, he raced a six-horse hitch through the streets at 2:00 A.M., actually speeding up as he swung into the livery stable where he had rented them. One animal hit a door post and was killed. Remarking that the animal was worth only 100 dollars, Ogilvy nevertheless gave the livery operator 1,000 dollars, explaining that the balance was for damage to the paint on the door.

At his ranch one day, Ogilvy recklessly decided to see if his buckboard team could jump a wide irrigation ditch. The answer was a resounding "No!"—one of the animals was killed when Ogilvy's rig smashed into the far bank of the ditch.

Ogilvy's horse capers were typical of the times—and of his origins. Wherever there were young Britons there were wild escapades involving horses. American cowboys didn't hesitate to put a horse through a grueling routine if the job demanded it but they had a greater respect for the animal's value than Britons.

Ogilvy may have escaped violent death by inches, but it was a mundane business deal that brought his downfall as a rancher. Having built the Ogilvy Ditch to serve his ranch and farmers upstream toward Greeley, he and a partner, Abner (Ab) Baker, contracted to build a major irrigation canal near Fort Morgan, a neighboring town.

The route chosen turned out to have hidden springs, which caused the horse-drawn scrapers to bog down in the muck. Desperately, Ogilvy secured a steam engine in Denver and finished the project by pulling the scrapers through the wet spots with a chain hooked to the steamer's belt pulley.

Nevertheless, the partners went belly up; Ogilvy had to sell his Crow Creek Ranch to pay his debts and move to a smaller ranch. His son, Jack, later a professor of English at the University of Colorado, said his father took the loss squarely.

"In those days," said Jack, "when you contracted to do something you were stuck with it." There's also some belief in Greeley that young Ogilvy, with excessive cash from home, was taken advantage of by some of the local promoters.

But there was always something wonderfully bizarre about Ogilvy, even in disaster. The story spread that Ogilvy had stolen the steam engine for his irrigation project and had spirited it from Denver at night, in the process weakening all the wooden bridges for sixty miles. The story turned out to be half right—Ogilvy drove the machine at night not because of theft (he had paid for it) but to keep the sight of the great lumbering monster from panicking all the horses and cows along the route.

His personal economics didn't improve and it wasn't long before Ogilvy was a ditchrider, supervising the water flow for another irrigation company at 3 dollars a day. That actually wasn't bad pay during the financial panic of 1893—but scarcely adequate for a Scottish aristocrat.

But the family money kept coming, and his desire for action didn't abate. He enlisted in the Spanish-American War, only to be kept stateside to endure nothing worse than dysentery in Florida. But there was a better war on the way, and Ogilvy traded his American uniform for a British tunic to fight in the Boer War.

To get to South Africa, Ogilvy, now nearing forty, contracted to supervise the shipboard care of seven hundred mules being sent from New Orleans to Capetown (like all fighting armies of that time the British needed a steady flow of thousands of horses and mules as replacements for those killed in battle). He was proud of the fact that he lost fewer than ten animals on the trip.

He treated sick animals by having them lifted to the deck and giving them free run of the ship. Thus, when the ship arrived at Capetown there was a mule in the prow braying his delight at seeing dry land. The incident prompted the captain's disgust. "Mr. Ogilvy," he said, "you are going to destroy my reputation as a sailor."

Ogilvy soon was in the midst of the action, serving with a colonial unit called Brabant's Territorials. He dared the marksmanship of Mauser-armed Boers by serving as a messenger. Characteristically, he secured a horse so swift that he claimed the Boers always shot behind him when he delivered messages to front-line commanders. He was under fire for 180 days and was given a captain's rank. One story of his courage is preserved by the family. Asked by his commander to meet with a Boer unit waving a white truce flag in the distance, Ogilvy declined to take troopers with him. "If I take troops along they'll kill us all," he told his superior. "If I go alone they'll talk." He returned unharmed and was awarded the Distinguished Service Order.

After his brother, the ninth earl of Airlie, was killed in battle in the Boer War, Lyulph would have succeeded to the title except for two small reasons—his brother's two young sons, the older of whom would now be earl of Airlie, guided by his widowed mother and grandmother. Primogeniture was served.

So it was back to Colorado for Ogilvy, who began raising sheep on a farm south of Greeley. In 1902 he married Edith Boothroyd, of an English ranching family in the Colorado foothills near Loveland. Their son, Jack, was born in 1902 at La Salle, and a daughter, Blanche Edith Maude, was born two years later (she died in 1915). It was at this time that the wild remittance man in Ogilvy gave way to a responsible search for a livelihood. Lyulph took his family to Scotland to meet the family. He presented Edith with a tailored Ogilvy tartan skirt. But perhaps he was also cutting his family ties for good.

The next years, in any case, were hard ones. He moved from the Greeley area to Denver in 1907, having lost the farm, and in 1908 his wife died. By 1909 this Scottish aristocrat was living in straitened circumstances, drinking too much and working as a night watchman in the railroad yards. It was that year that Harry Tammen, co-owner of the flamboyant *The Denver Post*, hired him as a writer specializing in farm subjects. Tammen called him Lord Ogilvy even though Ogilvy wasn't entitled to use the title—a nephew was the real earl of Airlie.

Leaving his children in the care of the Boothroyd grandparents, Ogilvy went to work as a journalist, a job he held until his retirement in 1945. It was a new discipline, and, while Ogilvy was well educated, his writing—in longhand—was nearly indecipherable and drove editors to drink. At first he was assigned stories about two agricultural colonies the newspaper promoted. Neither flourished and Ogilvy concentrated on Western affairs and on farm writing. Joy Swift, a *Post* writer who sat beside Ogilvy in those days and firmly defines him as a remittance man, once asked him for some stories about Buffalo Bill (a friend from Ogilvy's drinking days) to retell to her nephew. Ogilvy thought a moment and said, "I'm afraid any story I might tell about Buffalo Bill wouldn't be proper for the ears of a small boy."

But he knew livestock, and his crusade for upgrading the breeding of animals—especially the use of British cattle breeds like the Aberdeen Angus he'd imported to his Crow Creek ranch—was effective. He helped expand the National Western Stock Show in Denver each January, a nationally known exposition that did much to improve Western livestock breeding—and still does.

During his ranching career—when money from home was ample—Ogilvy had spent thousands of dollars on all kinds of breeding projects. He even tried to develop dogs fast enough, and large enough, to kill the prairie wolves that caused heavy losses to cattle herds. He never succeeded. A dog, seemingly, could be bred fast or large—but not both.

"Captain Ogilvy did more to advance the quality of horses, cattle and dogs in Colorado than any other man of his time," said John Petrikin, a Greeley banker who handled some of the 300,000 dollars in Scottish estate money that passed through Ogilvy's hands. On Ogilvy's innate nobility, Petrikin, who stoutly endured his own lifetime handicap of lameness, observed admiringly, "Lyulph Ogilvy could drink more whiskey and stand on his feet a gentleman longer than any other man in Colorado."

Appropriate testimonial, indeed. The irrepressible Ogilvy wouldn't be stilled. He spent his last years with his son, Jack, in Boulder and it was here that he died in 1947. But instead of a eulogy, it is fitting to report—as far more typical of Ogilvy's lively spirit—the story of a "funeral" caper perpetrated in Denver many years earlier:

A great drunken party had ended the night before and Ogilvy painfully left his room at the Windsor to conduct some business. As he passed a funeral parlor he mused what blessed relief death might bring. And then he remembered a bet he had made with a drinking pal, a fellow remittance man, that Ogilvy would die first. Inspired, he entered the establishment and inquired the price of the open casket in the window, along with the cost of a good funeral. The proprietor declared the cost to be 1,000 dollars and he soon had his money. Details are hazy but word spread in Denver that Ogilvy, by this time snoring in the plush-lined casket in the display room, was dead.

His friends knew better, however, and decided to prolong the joke. They hired a wagon to carry the "body" in its casket down 16th Street to the Windsor. On the way, the wagon hit the curb, causing the casket to pop open, with an enraged Ogilvy sitting up to shout: "Take it easy!"

That caused the inevitable runaway, leaving the small parade of mourners without their lively corpse who, along with his casket, was dashed in a grand climax to the paving stones at 16th and Curtis in lower downtown Denver.

With his hangover cured, Ogilvy soon was back at the Windsor Bar, setting 'em up for his friends while police finally found the runaway horses in the vicinity of the Statehouse a mile away.

Ogilvy's son Jack debunked many stories about his father but not this one. "Apparently something like this really did happen," he said.

That was vintage Ogilvy. But like Prince Hal, when the time came to face the real challenges of life, he was more than equal to the task. A remittance man who put aside the joyous days of adventure and drinking, he became quite a remarkable man despite the handicaps he gave himself. How deeply he felt his weaknesses was implicit in his comment one day to a fellow *Post* reporter. Asked why he didn't indulge in criticism of his gaudy, sensationalist boss Harry Tammen, he replied, "When a man saves your life, you feel everlasting gratitude."

His reverses never dimmed his love of life. He was loyal to Britain to the end and always projected the aura of an upper class British gentleman. But his lifestyle bore testimony to a love of freedom and democracy as embodied in American values. He once admitted it, saying, "What I like best about this country is that you can saddle your own horse."

❖
_____

Definitions

"Remittance Man ... A person living abroad on funds sent from home, especially in former times."

—American Heritage Dictionary

Remittance Men ... "These latter were the ne'er-do-well offspring of titled families banished to the plains with regular remittances, to stay until they either disappeared or straightened up and returned home. The typical remittance man was usually besotted and anonymous."

—*William H. Forbis,*
The Cowboys

Succession ... "When land is considered as the means only of subsistence and enjoyment, the natural law of succession provides it [to] all the children of the family ... but when land was considered as the means, not of subsistence, merely, but of power and protection, it was thought better that it should descend undivided to one."

—*Adam Smith,*
The Land Laws

Primogeniture ... "Wherever the institution came from, its advantages to both the lord and the tenant in an unsettled state of society, where a man might any day have to keep his goods and land by his own sword, are sufficiently obvious. ... Primogeniture, accordingly, grew fast at the expense of other rules of descent.

It was imported into England full-grown, and here it obtained, strangely as it appears at first sight, a more complete and lasting success than anywhere else. ... Primogentiture not only drove its rivals into corners and became the common law of

English landed property, but has outlasted the abolition of the military tenures to which it was in the first instance confined."
—*Frederick Pollock,*
The Land Laws

Primogeniture ... "No study of the English landed family makes any sense unless the principle and practice of primogeniture is constantly borne in mind. It is something which went far to determine the behaviour and characteristics of both parents and children. ... Under such a system both the elder and the younger children suffered. The latter normally inherited neither title nor estate, unless one of them happened to be heir to his mother's property, and they were therefore inevitably downwardly mobile. ... "
—*Lawrence Stone,*
Family, Sex and Marriage in England

Primogeniture ... "In England [in medieval times] the eldest son took over the family farm, but in France and the Rhineland the law stated that all children had the same right to inherit. All the same, there was a tendency to let the eldest son take over the farm. ... "
—Encyclopedia Britannica

❖

CHAPTER 10

A Social Life at Any Price

It was a tense moment at Hays, Kansas, on July 4, 1876. Thirsty Americans and Britons were gathered to observe the holiday with glasses of ale, wine and whiskey at Tommy Drumm's Saloon, one of the better drinking establishments in western Kansas. But the issue before the house was deceptively convivial: An American had just proposed that they all join in singing the "Star Spangled Banner."

The Britons, mostly remittance men from the English colony of Victoria ten miles away, demurred. One of them observed that it would be improper for them to sing to "the blarsted Republic." He urged, instead, that they sing "God Save the Queen," which a drunken American turned into "God Shave the Queen," and the fight was on. Fists, chairs and bottles flew. Tommy's well-polished pub was in shambles and his patrons battered and bloodied.

Outnumbered but too drunk to care, the unrepentent British were driven to the basement, where peacemakers resumed negotiations, finally winning agreement that each side would take turns. The Americans went first, but after singing, "Oh, shay can you shee by zhee dawn's er'y light ... " it turned out they didn't know the second line. Further, they were singing to the tune of

"John Brown's Body." Bygones soon became bygones and the remaining celebrants drank quietly, nursing black eyes, skinned knuckles and tender noses.

An unusual event, to be sure, but the story shows how touchy Anglo-British relations could become on the frontier. It also suggests how numerous upper class British migrants really were on the Western plains and how devoted they were—as they had been in Britain—to social drinking, even if it meant rubbing shoulders with rowdy Americans. English-style clubs naturally were preferred, but a tavern, even an American one on the Fourth of July, was an acceptable substitute.

Although the frontier had a few famous clubs that catered to Britons and cultured East Coast investors on tour, most social drinking was done at the better class hotels. Denver's famous Windsor Hotel, British-financed and completed on June 23, 1880, immediately springs to mind. Distinguished visitors from afar were grateful to shed train soot or trail dust for the quiet luxury of the five-story Windsor, truly a posh caravansery on what was often called the Great American Desert—a misnomer that cattle and grain soon would drive into disuse. With its twenty-foot-high ceilings, good food and comfortable beds, the Windsor drew much praise. Even Rose Pender, an acid-tongued British diarist, approved of the carpeting—as well as the Windsor chef's variety of fresh-baked breads when she and her wealthy husband checked in at the Windsor in 1883.

Adjoining the Windsor's spacious lobby was a fifty-foot-long billiard room, a wine room and a splendid bar featuring a 90-inch by 120-inch mirror, quite large for that time. Much of Denver's history was transacted in the Windsor bar but women saw none of it; the bar was off-limits to them. But there was a separate dining room for women and children, and on the second floor was the large Cattlemen's Room restaurant where Rose Pender undoubtedly formed her favorable impression of the Windsor's bakery. The entrées were impressive: The Windsor maintained a staff of hunters to provide venison and other wild meat.

It was at the Windsor that the eighth earl of Airlie, one of Scotland's most distinguished financiers, established temporary headquarters in 1881 for a tour of his Scottish company's ranch investments. And it was in a room at the Windsor that same year that he died after contracting typhoid in New Mexico territory. His son, Lyulph, who accompanied him on the fatal tour, soon was running cattle and breaking horses on the Colorado lands his father had purchased. Ogilvy was a born clubman and the Windsor Bar became his club in Denver.

Nearly every major cattle shipping center had at least one hotel—often near the stockyards—where cattlemen gathered to swap stories and compare cattle prices. Because many of the West's early big ranches were financed by Britons or Scots, these visitors were frequent patrons and their insistence on comfort and cleanliness helped set standards when new hotels were built. Fort Worth, Wichita, Kansas City, Omaha, Calgary and Sheridan, Wyoming, all had favorite hangouts for cattlemen. And where the cattlemen gathered, the British investors—often younger sons with a stake from home—were in the thick of things.

The wave of peripatetic Britons began soon after the American Civil War. They traveled west by the hundreds for adventure or investment, especially when the great trail herds of Texas longhorns arrived in Kansas from the south and prompted a hotel-building boom. The Drovers Cottage in Abilene was one of the earliest—built in 1868. It was wood, had three stories and was described as vaguely Italianate. Hailed as the finest hotel on the plains—for a time, at least—the Drovers Cottage added another import from Texas beside cattle—a long veranda to the front, where patrons could tilt back their chairs and watch the goings-on in the busy cowtown street.

Quarantine lines, set by state regulation, were moved steadily westward as Texas fever was discovered in the herds driven north to intersect the railroads. The cattle frontier thus became mobile and whole towns moved with it. The Drovers Cottage, for example, was dismantled, loaded on flatcars at Abilene and reopened sixty miles farther west at Ellsworth. British investors began skipping Abilene for points west, where the action was. Soon, trail herds were pushed all the way to Montana, as the removal of Indians turned the rich northern grasslands over to cattle. The clubmen and their caterers soon followed.

Younger British sons, bred to believe that gentlemen must keep up appearances, often spent too much money and time at hotel and club bars. Their families' grubstakes were given in expectation that the sons would soon invest in the West. Many did so—and became gentleman entrepreneurs on the high plains of the Rockies, the sheep ranges of Australia or New Zealand, the tea plantations of South Asia or the orchards of British Columbia.

All too many of the migrants spent too much money re-creating the social and sport-minded trappings of home in the form of a men's club—an organization dating from the sixteenth century and owing some of its better qualities to the stern intellectualism of Dr. Samuel Johnson, Edmund Burke and Oliver Goldsmith—a trend modified later by the convivial addition of alcohol. Even Dr. Johnson once declared, "As soon as I enter the door of a tavern I experience an oblivion of care ... "

Clubs followed the Union Jack around the world and to odd corners of the United States and South America. In the 1960s there was such a club in South India. A stone building of classic architecture, it was a relic of British rule.

The dusty oak furniture, art-deco wall hangings and old copies of *Punch* bespoke a time when planters from England mingled with adventuring military officers and administrators from home, forgetting colonial burdens for an hour or two of conviviality. Images from Kipling crowded one's thoughts.

Even if a range country club was founded by Britons, most members were upwardly mobile American businessmen and ranchers, often from the East. They felt kinship with Britain and welcomed the tone and ready cash that upper class Britons gave in their establishments. The El Paso Club in Colorado Springs is a good example. Founded in 1877 by several Englishmen and their Anglophile friends, the El Paso vies with San Francisco's Bohemian Club as the first permanent men's social club west of Chicago. Noted for its mineral springs and healthy climate, Colorado Springs was virtually a British spa and was known as Li'l Lunnon. Marshall Sprague, the club's chronicler, explained, "The male club became an absolute necessity in England in the eighteenth century and it is not surprising that, in October 1877, Dr. S.E. Solly and other Englishmen ... felt the need to organize the El Paso Club." Sprague might have added that the town was "dry" by order of its founder, General William Jackson Palmer, and having a place to store one's bottles was regarded as a necessity.

After several years of occupying upstairs rooms in downtown Colorado Springs, the El Paso Club in 1891 purchased a large brick residence, which it expanded and still occupies, more than one hundred years later. And there is progress: the club now has one woman member.

Leather chairs in the reading room were, of course, de rigeur, and a long table featured newspapers and quality magazines like *The Century* and even *Blackwood's*, delivered from Edinburgh. The second floor had a pool room with five billiard tables and card rooms for poker, whist, piquet and twenty-one. Ladies were permitted only at magnificent formal balls, although a small ladies' dining room was installed in 1910.

British decorum prevailed only until the club began admitting the roistering gold millionaires, coming down from Cripple Creek to spend their wealth. A savage billiard cue duel was reported on one occasion, broken windows on another—certainly not the acts of gentlemen. But even in its wildest moments the El Paso Club never approximated the image of gun-toting, chair-flying violence projected by popular historians of the Wild West. El Paso members appreciated more cultured pranks, as when a bachelor member wired from the East Coast that he was bringing home a bride and would introduce her to the club. His bride turned out to be a lovely Italian girl—not in flesh but carved in marble. The statue, named Mrs. Pomeroy for her purchaser, today kneels chastely in the east bay window of the reading room as she has for a century.

Perhaps the cattle country's most famous men's club—also with a strong mixture of British culture and even a few remittance men as visitors—was the Cheyenne Club in Cheyenne, Wyoming. In recent times it was chosen as the apparent setting for the movie, *The Cheyenne Social Club*, which was mistaken when it cast a club very much like the Cheyenne Club as a brothel. This is simply untrue, according to historian Agnes Wright Spring. She pointed out that it was, after all, the Victorian era, and if gentlemen formed a club they weren't about to compromise their reputations by admitting women of ill-repute. There were hotels for that sort of thing.

The brick three-story Cheyenne Club opened in April 1881, in what is now downtown Cheyenne. The club served excellent formal dinners, stocked only the best imported wines and cigars and dictated strict rules of behavior covering drinking, conduct in the billiard room and the general decorum of members. One member was suspended for five months for calling another a "vile" name. Enlarged in 1884 to accommodate its 170 members (half of them Cheyenne residents), the club included a post office and fourteen bedrooms. It had electricity; its dining room was thirty feet square. Later, a telegraphic ticker tape kept members apprised of the markets. Games played for money were forbidden, although what members did in their own rooms was their own business.

Most of the members were wealthy Americans, some veteran cattlemen of the territory and some polished New Englanders with

Cheyenne Club, a social center for cattlemen in southeast Wyoming, drew many English gentleman visitors to its excellent dining and wine cellar. Rules against rowdy conduct were strictly enforced. (Photo courtesy of the Denver Public Library, Western History Department.)

investments in cattle. But the few British members—remittance men or not—made up in class what they lacked in numbers. Among them were brothers Moreton and Richard Frewen, wealthy landed gentry from Sussex, who for a time claimed their grazing lands in northeast Wyoming were larger than all of Ireland. Moreton Frewen was the persuasive promoter of ranch stock among upper class British investors and frequently hosted his titled visitors at the club and at his Cheyenne guest house which served as a stopping place for visitors arriving by train to visit his ranch. Frewen, you will recall, died a pauper in London in 1924.

The most distinguished international member of the Cheyenne Club was Horace Plunkett, the third son of the sixteenth Lord Dunsany. Born of an Anglo-Irish family he attended Eton and Oxford and, at twenty-five, migrated to the American West with a family nest egg. In ten years he made a great deal of money in cattle in Wyoming. Club lore insists that Plunkett's dexterity was exhibited by playing an expert game of tennis while calling to the sidelines his moves in a chess game, which he also won. Returning to Ireland, he became a major force in Irish agricultural reform, largely because of his Western ranching experience. He was knighted for his statesmanship in the struggles over Irish independence. Superficially, he paralleled the lives of many Western remittance men with this difference: He was broadly educated and exceptionally self-disciplined.

Other men's clubs often drew comment from British guests. William French, like Plunkett an Anglo-Irish younger son, became a successful New Mexico cattleman and wrote an account of his American career. Attending a cattlemen's convention in Denver, he took special note of the Denver Club, where he was a guest of Alfred Rowe, the famous English cattle baron from Texas, who died in the *Titanic* disaster. In its early days the Denver Club, founded in 1880, occupied a splendid Victorian mansion in Denver's financial district. Sold to the Murchison interests of Texas, the club now has moved twenty stories up, atop a nondescript office building on the same site. Its atmosphere is gone, but a member can see in the distance the mountains and plains that nourished infant Denver with gold, cattle and sheep.

Estes Park and Glenwood Springs, with large hotels, became popular British rest stops in Colorado because of their scenery and recreation. Theodore Roosevelt, who, as a youth, had ranched for two years in Dakota Territory, returned to his beloved West when he was the country's chief executive. He spent several days at Glenwood Springs to hunt big game and enjoy the luxurious Hotel Colorado, another spa built with British monetary assistance. Like so many Britons and Easterners, he was captivated by the wonders of the West, not least its health-giving air and scenery. Not surprisingly, the chief organizer of the still-famous mineral springs spa at Glenwood was a wealthy, Princeton-educated Easterner, Horace Devereux, who tapped British investors for 250,000 dollars to help build his project. As British travel increased, Devereux and his friends added a polo field and race track.

Railroads spurred the influx of tourists. The Burlington's arrival in northern Wyoming put Sheridan on the international map in 1893. The three-story Sheridan Inn became a popular gathering place as young Britons arrived by the score to play polo, invest in ranch land and establish an active social life in the spas and in the homes of local British ranchers. Buffalo Bill, whose Wild West show had played London, must have thrilled the dudes when he made an occasional stopover at the Sheridan Inn.

Neighboring Miles City, Montana, was equally popular with a variety of travelers. Its Macqueen House was popular with cattlemen who gathered for annual conventions and stayed there during business trips. But the Macqueen House found special favor with Britons by expanding its menu to include loin of beef and Yorkshire pudding during the Christmas season.

Greater British purity was maintained in the hotels and clubs of Canada, which, after all, had never rebelled against the mother country. Victoria, the beautiful capital of British Columbia, has a deserved reputation for being more English than the English. Its appeal for British visitors at the turn of the century was tremendous. According to historian Gwen Hayball:

> ... the remittance man was easily recognized by the "honest working man." If it was possible to get by without working, they

would be seen in their English cut tweeds, smoking the fashionable briar pipe, strolling about the rooms of the Empress Hotel or taking their ease at the Union Club. The majority were content to live on their periodic allowances which they usually collected from the General Delivery wicket at the Post Office."

One can imagine similar delights when young men like these entered the Garry Club far to the east, in Winnipeg. Manitoba didn't offer any breathtaking mountain scenery but members of the Garry Club made their own fun with polo, hockey, club fights and boat racing. There was the usual friction between older members and the supercilious new arrivals from Britain. As one contemporary noted:

The newcomers wore Old School ties and spoke with an Oxford accent, and these were regarded [by Canadian natives] as earmarks of the 'remittance man,' a species definitely suspect. ... According to popular belief they had been booted out of Britain ... with the promise of a monthly allowance if they stayed put and kept the family name off the police blotter.

But they thrived on club life and one young Briton endeared himself to his peers (if not his elders) by a prank he played at the Garry's turkish bath. Peering in the door of the bath, he saw on the slab an elderly gentleman receiving a massage from the proprietor.

Pushing the masseur aside, he cried, "Here, put a little life into it," and began slapping the customer's pink and ample buttocks with stinging vigor. The victim arose with ponderous dignity and stalked out of the room with a look of bitter disapproval.

"Do you know who that was?" asked the masseur.

"Haven't the foggiest," was the reply.

"That," said the proprietor, "was the premier of Manitoba and, in future, kindly keep your hands to yourself."

World War I decimated the Garry Club. Junior members enlisted to a man and several died in France. Few returned to Winnipeg, preferring to settle down to marriage and jobs in Britain.

The Ranchman's Club of Calgary was Alberta's first private club and, besides cattlemen, had Northwest Mounted policemen as charter members. By serving in the NWMP, young troopers qualified for homesteads and, finishing their service, became ranchers. The club thus was a good place to get started. Male members of the Calgary club surrendered in 1925, when females were allowed limited access by the side door.

Gambling was an evil in some clubs in the cattle country. A wealthy visiting Briton loaned a card sharp 500 dollars to enter a game at one of the Foothills clubs in Alberta. When the professional gambler had won 20,000 dollars from the Briton the manager stepped in and declared the game illegal—with no debts owing. He learned later that the Englishman, clinging to his code of honor, had sold enough cattle and horses to satisfy the debt.

Seasoned stockmen regarded their clubs as a deserved reward for their successful struggle against the elements. But for new arrivals the clubs that sprang up in the new towns all over the Canadian west signaled a wasteful excess. In the view of historian Patrick Dunae: "Capital that should have been invested in acres and ploughs, melted away in all kinds of riotous living. ... Pyramids of empty champagne bottles for the first and probably the last time rose upon the prairie." Club life has changed everywhere—partly due to the admittance of women—but Britain, where it all started, still is a bastion of companionable, clubbish men. A young author from British Columbia recently was invited to dinner at the famous Travelers Club in London, a comfortable masonry pile with twenty-foot ceilings, starched linen tablecloths and heavy silver. He could scarcely believe his good fortune.

"It's the club," he said admiringly, "where Phileas Fogg started his trip in *Around the World in 80 Days!*" That, of course, was a fictional adventure by Jules Verne, later rewritten for the movies. And Fogg's club was the Reform Club—also on Pall Mall, naturally. But if you believe strongly enough it doesn't matter. While clubs were a drain on the pocketbooks of globe-trotting young Britons, they were also a great comfort. No doubt they satisfied the yearning for happiness, however transitory. As Dr. Johnson noted, in a good tavern one's troubles magically disappear—at least for a time.

But for the destitute remittance man there was little chance of club membership. A hotel bar had to suffice—but only when the mail had brought a check from home. Bizarre stories of self-imposed isolation and stiff-lipped independence still echo in the Australian outback and in the lonely valleys of the American West and Canada. The tales outlive their protagonists—but just barely. A few frail remittance men still were alive in the 1990s, scattered worldwide, with limited social contact and few friendships.

Until recently two lonely brothers lived—that's right, *lived*—in a station wagon in the upper reaches of the River Murray of South Australia. They replaced the car with a new model whenever their remittance checks from Britain permitted a trade-in. Periodically they moved to a new location when boredom set in amidst the billibongs, gum trees and spinifex.

British Columbia was home to hundreds of remittance men eking out a solitary existence by raising a few cattle or running a small fruit and vegetable farm after the money from home stopped coming. Many successful Britons still retire to the mild climate of the Canadian West Coast and gather at their hotels and clubs to swap yarns of their worldly experiences. But few can match the legendary tale of the unsociable remittance man who went native and lived like a wild animal in Canada's deep pine forests. At least, that's the story. Was Sasquatch an English remittance man? Don't be surprised. After all, Tarzan was an English aristocrat for whom Edgar Rice Burroughs conjured up the name, Lord Greystoke. Perhaps after he left Africa …

❧
———————

Dudes Meet the Class of ".45"

Occasionally [in Montana] there would be a so-called remittance man—college bred and maybe the son or relative of one of
the owners of the outfit who would come out for the summer,
that would feel superior to the cowhands. Not all of them tried
to show their superiority, but if they did the cowboys really gave
them a bad time. I knew of one such who would always try to use
big words and then follow up by explaining what he meant in
more common or understandable language. Finally the boys got
so whenever this individual would use a big word somebody
would scream out, "Where did it go?" Somebody would point,
generally to the corner of the ceiling and somebody else would
whip out a six shooter and whang away at it … as a result some
of our old log buildings had .45 slugs peppered all over.
              —*quoted by Mark Brown and W. R. Felton*
                             Before Barbed Wire

❖

CHAPTER 11

Fun and Games
in the Canadian West

Valhalla, the great hall of heroes in ancient Norse mythology, provided slain warriors bliss in the hereafter. They dined daily on the flesh of a slaughtered wild boar that mysteriously was brought to life again each morning. In an eerie parallel, scores of British remittance men found their Valhalla in Western Canada where they only dreamed of glory as they lazily drank themselves to death, their whiskey glasses refilled—almost as magically—by remittance checks from home.

There were no mighty shields on the walls of the Canadian Valhalla, but there might be stuffed moose and elk heads above the bars of the taverns where remittance men did their persistent drinking. Their family crests might display swords and other implements of war but their military exploits were dubious— heroes to no one except their mothers.

British families thought their remittance mailings were putting their sons on their feet, training them to achieve great things in the western wilderness. But Canadians knew better. The unfortunate young gentlemen, trained in classics and athletic sports (but in little else) at Eton, Rugby or other public schools, all too often were reduced to cadging drinks at the bar, promising to repay the loan as soon as the next check arrived from home.

The remittance man quickly achieved unenviable rank as a prime source of Western Canadian humor.

Except for Quebec, Canada is a British mapmaker's exercise reflecting Britain's eighteenth- and nineteenth-century political compromises. Demographically, it resembles a nonsensical, horizontal Chile with the vast majority of its twenty-five million people snuggled up against the American border—a geographic bulwark against the powerful northward thrust of the newly independent United States. Britain continued its protective and economic support after granting dominion status to Canada in 1867. As part of the British Commonwealth, Canada loyally supported the mother country in war.

Anglo loyalty and cultural ties remained strong even after the railroads began dumping tens of thousands of European peasants and American migrants into the western regions. But the conquest of the West created a tough, independent frontier mindset which became Canada's own unique contribution to the Anglo world. The homesteaders, ranchers and merchants had worked hard and suffered a great deal for their stake and now, savoring land ownership and free western enterprise, they silently vowed never to resubmit to the British class system they had left behind.

That's why young British gentlemen routinely received a shock when they got off the train at Winnipeg, Medicine Hat or Calgary. They weren't addressed as Sir or Your Lordship. Also, no one looked after them. They were free to sink or swim by their own abilities. If they got bilked in a land deal, tough luck.

But for some reason—perhaps because the British upper classes invested so heavily in western Canada—the Canadian response to foolish gentlemen immigrants dwelt more on humor than on verbal savaging. In Australia and in the United States the naïve newcomer was apt to discover that his friends disappeared, or even turned hostile, the moment his money ran out.

In Canada the remittance man could be regarded as a scalawag but still a likable fellow—more an object of cheerful humor than strong dislike. Such a view helps explain the wealth of remittance man humor, which developed early and still prompts Western Canadians to repeat such stories nearly as often as they tell tall tales about their region's fabled chinook winds.

So durable is the theme that the Canadian novelist Eric Nicol recently wrote the best-selling book *Dickens of the Mounted*, purporting to be the "long-lost" letters of Frank Dickens, third son of the famous writer, Charles Dickens. Young Frank Dickens actually did endure the miserable life of a money-short remittance man. Born in 1844, he was educated in a succession of places, including Germany and, while he was fairly bright, he stuttered and failed the exams for entry to medical school. His father stepped in and used his influence to win his son an appointment to the Bengal Mounted Police in India. Frank failed that, too, and in 1874 he was appointed (again with the help of his family) as an inspector in the Northwest Mounted Police (NWMP) in western Canada. It wasn't long before his superiors were reporting to Ottawa that he was, in their words, "lazy, alcoholic and unfit to be an officer in the NWMP."

He failed to anticipate trouble with the Indians. On one occasion he allowed his men to be trapped in a building besieged by hostiles; they escaped only through the lucky discovery of boats on a nearby river. Such conduct led the authoritative *Canadian Encyclopedia* to this harsh indictment: "Dickens can be blamed for worsening relations between the Blackfoot and the NWMP and for the growing antipathy of the officer cadre toward Englishmen."

Retiring from the NWMP in 1886, he died the same year of a stroke on the eve of a lecture tour, in Moline, Illinois—his first stop. Kindly Moline residents paid for his burial when Dickens' brothers and sisters declined to send money to have his body returned to England. By then the family had divided their illustrious father's estate (Charles Dickens died in 1870) and apparently had little interest in their wandering brother, Frank. (He had, of course, already squandered his share.)

This then became a factual base for the grand semifictional spoof by Eric Nicol in 1989. Nicol even turns a neat Dickensian phrase with this beginning: "It was not the best of times, it was not the worst of times, it was Ottawa." From Ottawa young Frank gets lost as he searches for his Mountie post, falls off his horse backward when he finally meets his commanding officer, proves incapable of dealing with Indians and drinks to excess—

the perfect icon of remittance men. Upon one occasion in Alberta, when superiors have seized and dumped illegal American liquor shipped to the Indians, Frank falls to his knees and joins his enlisted men in eating up the whiskey-soaked snow, citing regulations which specified only that a Mountie must not drink while on duty.

It's strange that Hollywood, in its search for glamor in the history of the Mounted Police, never hit upon Frank Dickens as a comic subject. Imagine the fun W. C. Fields could have had in the title role as he staggered from saloon to saloon, besmirching the Mounties' reputation for always getting their man.

When Hollywood did discover the Mounties it was for the wrong reasons. There had never been much romance in the tough, paramilitary corps sent west to keep order after rebellious factions on the Western plains threatened bloody mayhem. But neither were they supermen. They sometimes retreated from outlaws and Indians, a tactic the real and the fictional Frank Dickens heartily endorsed.

What the Mounties deserve great credit for is their quiet and effective work in understanding and seeking friendship with native cultures in an area larger than Europe. Because Canadian authorities organized the Mounties to put down French unrest in the West there was a strong British ethnic strain in the recruits, many of them migrants from good families in England. They were well educated and did double duty as justices of the peace as well as policemen in the remote tundra. So it is no accident that the Mounties had no blood baths comparable to the American disaster at the Little Big Horn. When possible they cooperated with the Indians. In fact, Americans can thank the Mounties for gradually strangling the insidious liquor pipeline from the states. The enemy was not natives but unscrupulous American liquor traders seeking to swap Canadian tribes out of everything they owned, debauching and brutalizing them in the process.

But American moviegoers were ready for tales of romance involving the NWMP, later renamed as the much more dashing Royal Canadian Mounted Police. And that's how Hollywood dished it out—manly and romantic. Mounted Police officers from Ottawa regularly went to Hollywood. Horrified at the mushy love stories being put on celluloid they hoped that, as technical advisers, they might avert even worse perversions of the script writers.

Scores of movies glorified the Mounties and Mountie comic strips filled U.S. newspapers. Musical compositions appeared. The craze probably reached a peak in 1936 in *Rose Marie* in which Nelson Eddy, resplendently redcoated, took Jeanette MacDonald in his arms as they sang "Indian Love Call." Other towering heroics were heaped on the Mounties by Gary Cooper, Robert Preston, Alan Ladd and Shirley Temple. But nobody played Frank Dickens.

Actually, the main remittance man theme in Canadian humor involves dashing young Britons who landed on the cattle ranges with an expectation of riding to the hounds while their "cow servants" rounded up and branded their herds out on the prairie. Many of them showed gritty courage along with their stupidity, a mixture that draws a sort of head-shaking admiration in the literature of the western Canadian provinces. It is the praise one reserves for a lovable dog that chases cars or barks at the moon. Many of these men salvaged something in maturity by recklessly going off to die for England in World War I.

Canada's remittance men followed patterns similar to those below the border. But for every failed remittance man, there were dozens of hard-working British men and women who grew calluses on their hands by joining Germans, Slavs, Scandinavians and Americans in making the land produce wheat, cattle, sheep and other farm income. In fact, it was American herds driven north from Montana that built the core of Alberta's cattle industry, supplemented by purebred breeding stock from Britain.

Canadian purists didn't like the non-British influx. The eastern Europeans, especially, clumped into colonies and maintained non-Anglo cultural, religious and political views. Many refused military conscription, leading to harassment of Germans in World War I and the remigration of hundreds of Mennonites from Canada to Mexico in the 1920s.

So immigration became a political battleground. But through it all British arrivals retained top priority because their family money—even if squandered—was desperately needed in the unincorporated west. In addition to other Europeans, large numbers of Frenchmen had moved west with the fur trade and had taken Indian wives. The resultant offspring, called Metis (half-breeds), established communities that, tending toward Roman Catholicism and the French language, constantly threatened rebellion against the lightly governed British administrative structures in the West. A combination of uprisings by the Metis, American pressures and Indian troubles relating to westward expansion, made the Northwest Mounted Police vital to peace in the Northwest territories.

British Canadians, of course, didn't feel threatened by their own kind, even when the immigrant was a remittance man who spent his money foolishly. It all added up to money in the bank for the struggling businessmen who serviced the ventures until their losses forced the newcomers to sell to better farmers and go back to Britain. Canada's immigration posters, circulating in Britain, weren't specifically aimed at tricking young nabobs out of their inheritance but that often was the result.

Many stories centered around the mistakes the young Britons made because they were untrained. One such story insists that when a rancher sent his British pupil out to round up the sheep the young man didn't come back until after dark, complaining that the long-eared sheep had been "deucedly" hard to catch. The rancher examined his pen and found jackrabbits mixed in with the flock. An unlikely occurrence—but the ranch country revels in tall tales.

Even in the most hilarious stories there is a lesson or an element of truth that shouldn't be overlooked, and the storyteller was always ready to concede that many a bumbling remittance man matured into a useful citizen, putting his critics to shame.

One of the harshest critics was Frank G. Carpenter. Writing at the turn of the century, he described the daily scene in Calgary, Alberta:

> These remittance men get so much money every month, or every quarter, and most of them spend it in drinking and carousing. Many are 'ne'er-do-wells,' and they fall lower and lower, relying entirely on their remittances to keep them going. I know, for instance, one son of an English lord, whom you may see almost any day here hanging over a bar and another who has ducal

blood in his veins, who will gladly borrow a quarter of you if he strikes you in the lean days prior to the next remittance.

Carpenter conceded, however, that other young men "keep themselves straight," invest money wisely and "make it breed like Australian rabbits, but at the same time they are full of sport and spend freely."

One of Carpenter's best stories is probably apocryphal but it has become part of Alberta's ranching lore. Carpenter's tale centers on William Edward (Billy) Cochrane, son of a British admiral. A Calgary banker who visited Cochrane's ranch was shocked to find Cochrane sitting on a corral fence watching a deadly fight between two valuable bulls Cochrane had just imported from Scotland. The banker climbed to a seat on the fence and, as he witnessed the struggle, he said, "Why, Billy, if you do not separate those bulls one will kill the other." "Let them kill," was the reply. "This is the real thing. It is better than any Spanish bullfight and I would give a bull any day to see it."

A well-dressed group on C.P.R. station platform at Medicine Hat includes a Northwest Mounted Policeman. September 9, 1891. (Photo courtesy of the Glenbow Archives, Calgary, Alberta, Canada. Photo #NA-529-1.)

After an hour of combat, with Cochrane urging his bulls to greater effort, one of them gored and killed his rival. The banker decried the waste of valuable stock but Cochrane replied: "Oh! It don't matter at all. We have got to have some sport. We must have something to add to the life of the ranch."

This same Cochrane outgrew the need for blood sport in his corrals to become a prominent stockman in Alberta livestock circles. His cattle profits enabled him to accompany his wife on winter trips to England, where they renewed old friendships and enjoyed the sophisticated life in London. A remittance man, yes, and a successful one who soon earned his own way in Canada.

Carpenter also told about Dickie Bright, grandson of the doctor for whom Bright's disease was named. Learning that his father, also a doctor, was arriving from England to check on his son's success in cattle ranching, the young man panicked. He had spent his remittances wastefully.

Desperation produced a strategy. Dickie borrowed 1,000 cattle from a good-humored neighbor for a day and a night. When his father saw the herd he was so pleased he gave the young man 10,000 dollars to expand his operations. Dickie then explained the animals had to be hurried out on the range again. When he had dissipated the 10,000 dollars he sent word to England the animals had died of cold and disease. His ruse was exposed and he was called home.

Remittance men tricked their families out of money in a variety of ways. One submitted to his parents the falsehood that he had required expert surgery and that the surgeon, brought from Toronto, had billed him thousands of dollars which he couldn't pay. Another found a sister willing to pay his ranching debts so, in connivance with a merchant, he had his sister double-billed for his expenses, splitting the profits with the merchant. Amusing as such stories are, they really teach a lesson about parental stupidity, masking certain failure about which it is better, looking back, to laugh than to cry.

The desperate idea that a family could send a callow son thousands of miles from home and expect him to succeed reflected faith in Britain's economy. Given the nation's immense nineteenth-century global reach (the English pound sterling ruled the land nearly as effectively as the English Navy ruled the seas), the strategy made some sense. But the sons were usually immature and, despite the settlers' efforts to picture them as rich men's sons, many were simply middle class boys who were well educated as gentlemen but were miserably unprepared when the remittances stopped.

Britain's economy, no longer agricultural, was suffering and emigration was needed. But the response was so disorganized that it almost resembled Europe's Children's Crusade of 1212, in which thousands of children were sent on a disastrous mission to conquer the Holy Land. Most of the young Britons, while a few years older, were scarcely better prepared for the gauntlet of wilderness and scheming con men than Europe's children had been 850 years earlier in the Mideast.

One hard-bitten Canadian, having outrageously overcharged a newcomer in a sight-unseen ranch sale, silently cursed his luck (he told his friends later) when the young Briton revealed that he had kept additional sums in reserve for the farm's buildings and other improvements—which, of course, did not exist. But the Canadian gladly would have dreamed up a few structures to throw into the deal if he hadn't been too hasty in closing it.

Poking fun at remittance men became a cottage industry. Bob Edwards, a Scottish immigrant newspaperman with a flair for satire, was typical of the Alberta newspapermen who pilloried the young Britons mercilessly.

He wrote of one flagrant boozer who, learning his parents were coming to visit his hovel, talked a prosperous neighbor into lending him his ranch house for the visit. The neighbor agreed, helped the young man to sober up and even pretended to be the butler, serving the parents nothing stronger than tea.

When the mother prepared to leave she said to her son: "By the way, James, what is a jaggon?"

"A what, Mother?"

"A jaggon. I overheard your cowboys saying that it was a wonder you hadn't a jaggon."

"Oh, yes," said Jimmy, recovering his composure. "A jaggon is a white shirt and they were doubtless wondering why I did not don a white shirt in your honor."

Cartoonists had a field day. Bob Edwards' *Eye-Opener* carried a sketch of a penniless remittance man, his collar and trouser seat in the firm grasp of a bartender, being frog-marched into the street from a tavern. But the next panel shows the same pair on the day when the remittance has arrived. "A brandy and soda and be quick about it," says the Briton and the obsequious bartender is falling all over himself to comply.

Such savage humor, along with unhappy letters sent home by young men, brought a reaction. Families realized some of the advertisements that induced them to pay tuition to a ranch school were little more than confidence games that took the money and gave their sons little education. British writers, editors and educators realized the tragedy and made strenuous efforts, both in Britain and abroad, to improve the training the young gentlemen received, particularly in farming.

A common pattern was to start a colony. With their penchant for organization, moneyed Britons often sold legitimate memberships or shares in overseas land schemes that provided training as well as farmland. One of the most ambitious was Cannington Manor, a bit of sporting England transplanted to Saskatchewan soil. Here young lords hunted foxes, raced their horses, played cricket and paid for huge quantities of machinery and other farm equipment with which to raise wheat and other crops.

Named for a place in Somersetshire, England, Cannington Manor was first settled in 1882 with construction of a twenty-one-room manor house that served as a center for games and socializing by the colonists and their families. An Anglican Church and individual estates soon followed, and Cannington Manor prospered for a time, reaching a population of 150 by 1888. But nobody farmed and, when the railroad located its line eight miles to the south in 1890, most of the merchants moved southward, dooming Cannington Manor. Very similar stories are told elsewhere in Canada and the United States. Because they spoke English the new settlers found little difficulty relocating to more prosperous sites and vocations. Many, of course, went back to Britain nearly broke.

But even bitter critics of the young migrants appreciated the newcomers' contributions to community growth in western

Canada, both in money and importation of good quality live-stock. And a minority became effective administrators in government and industry.

Many historians feel remittance men were undeserving of the joking stories about their mistakes. They proved able in many ways and, given friendship and good supervision, made substantial contributions to the frontier. It was the untrained youth—or the hard cases whose lives had been warped before they left Britain—who gave the breed a bad name.

Many of them were nearing midlife when World War I broke out in 1914. Perhaps to salvage something of their dissipation they joined British forces in France in comparatively large numbers, leaving the mountains and prairies of Canada and the western United States to serve the mother country. It's a fact that the sons of the upper class families died in greater percentages than other British classes in that war—comparatively more of them enlisted.

Many literate Canadians today urge the families of such pioneering men to be proud of their ancestry. Even as early as 1917, one of their harshest critics noted their service on French battlefields and observed, "They may be green but they're not yellow."

If Canada became their Valhalla most of them certainly earned it with suffering and sometimes with notable success. Valhalla, after all, was for fallen heroes, possibly including those felled by strong drink. And they had—at least for a time—given it the old public school try.

❖
———————

The London Scene versus
San Angelo

Born in 1879 in Ireland, Clodagh de la Poer Beresford, daughter of the fifth marquess of Waterford, wrote a book in 1957 to cap a long and full life. She enjoyed travels in Mexico—where she descended in a mine dressed as a man—and spent part of her life in Texas, where she ranched with her husband, Claud Anson, at San Angelo. She enjoyed Texas hospitality, but her class upbringing triumphed and she returned to her first love, London's brilliant social scene.

In her book *Victorian Days*, Lady Anson gave this insight on aristocratic marriages:

> Once you were married ... you had to be "good" or "bad." If you were good you behaved nicely and had an extremely dull life. If you were bad, of course there were heaps of thrilling adventures. The racing set, who were alluded to as the "Smart Set" in the newspapers, had a good deal of fun and notoriety. They had wild affairs with each other's wives and husbands, and as divorce was out of the question, lived with each other quite indiscriminately, and made no secret of it. ... Their first baby generally was legitimate, but after that their family varied in descent in the most amazing way. This was so taken for granted among the "Fast Set," that if two (unwed) people did really love each other and remained faithful, their liaison was looked on as being as respectable and dull as a marriage.
> —*Clodagh de la Poer Beresford*
> Victorian Days

Farther north, young emigrants had little or no contact with the opposite sex. One Oxford expatriate reported in 1905 from Alberta that he had not even seen a woman in nearly three years.

✤

CHAPTER 12

Refuge in Mexico

Anyone asked to guess which highborn son of an aristocratic British family would grow up to become a hard-drinking remittance man in the American West would almost certainly bypass Lord Delaval James de la Poer Beresford. He was a weakwilled blue blood born in 1862 to an Anglo-Irish family whose hardy ancestors had been powerful land owners in southern Ireland for many generations.

They were the lords of Waterford, a county on the south coast once ruled by Norsemen and famous today for its fine crystal. The Beresfords were both clever politicians and good landlords to the tenants who farmed thousands of acres surrounding the family estate at Curraghmore. But dirt farmers they were not. When a Beresford mounted a horse, it was not to drive cattle but to follow the hounds in pursuit of a fox.

The family's oldest known roots are through the de la Poer line, dating back nearly a millenium. The de la Poers were followers of William the Conqueror when he left Normandy for England in 1066. After subduing the English, William's Norman barons invaded Ireland and within a century held most of the island. A de la Poer arrived at Curraghmore in 1170, and it has been home ever since, for more than eight centuries. King William

I and his successors believed in rewarding loyalty (for future fealty as well as the past), and Ireland soon filled up with Norman-Irish noblemen. The de Burgos became Irish Burkes, the Blanchettes the Plunketts and a deserving royal servant became one of the biggest landowners of all under his generic name, Butler.

Many de la Poers adopted the name Powers. But the branch that didn't change included a tough-minded woman who married into the Beresford line in 1717 and simply annexed her new family name to her old one. She thus founded the dynasty that produced "Delaval James de la Poer Beresford," a colorful, convention-defying remittance man on the American frontier.

Compared to the de la Poers, the Beresfords were upstarts whose affluent, landed status was established by a Beresford who fought against the French at Agincourt in 1415. His loyalty, earned with broadsword and dagger in one of the bloodiest battles of the Middle Ages, was generously rewarded.

But the Beresfords owed their real rise to social prominence to an accident of sex thee hundred years later. In 1717, the prestigious de la Poers were without a male heir to retain the family's extensive lands. Daughter Catherine rose to the occasion. She persuaded the Irish Parliament to give her the Barony of la Poer as a dowry and a lure for suitors. Then she picked out a husband who happened to be named Beresford and stipulated that their offspring be named de la Poer Beresford. And they were.

In a bit of irony, the need for linguistic brevity undid Catherine's intent. The family soon was known as just Beresford, even though birth certificates carried the full name.

The couple created a splendid genetic inheritance but young Delaval didn't get much of it. His older brothers exemplified the family derring-do around the world, but Delaval wallowed in the soft upper class atmosphere of servants, fine clothes and large comfortable mansions. He was poorly prepared for the long jump from green, lush Ireland to the tan, dusty American frontier.

He shared the family fondness for good whiskey, but he did not have the same drive as his brawling ancestors, who were blessed with Irish wit and loved practical jokes. The family virtuoso in this regard was Lord Henry (1811–1859), Delaval's uncle, who was often called the Mad Marquess or the Wild Lord of Waterford.

Lord Henry's eccentricities are still notable. He once rented a hunting lodge from another family and then amused himself by using his pistol to shoot out the eyes of the family portraits on the walls. On another occasion he caused a near-heart attack by trussing a donkey beneath the covers of a fellow patron's bed at an inn where he was staying. He once offered a railway company full compensation for damages if the company would smash two locomotives together at top speed so he could witness the spectacle. The railroad politely refused.

One of his most elaborate pranks involved a circuit-riding minister, Lord Henry's hunting dogs and some highly aromatic aniseed oil, a flavoring used in liqueur. He covertly daubed the oil on the hooves of the minister's horse. Giving the man of God a good start he then gave his hunting pack a strong sniff of anise and set them loose, galloping along delightedly as the dogs—in full voice—chased the frightened divine over hill and dale.

Lord Henry also took suicidal chances. He once leaped from the deck of his yacht to chase his cap into a raging sea in the Bay of Biscay. The captain lowered a boat and miraculously found his master a mile astern, half-drowned but clutching his cap.

His actual death was virtually self-inflicted. Proud of his horsemanship, he rode his mounts hard and over bizarre jumps. He once took a mount over a fully set dinner table without damaging even the delicate, sparkling Waterford crystal. But on March 29, 1859, his luck ran out. After pushing his horse to near exhaustion he forced the poor animal to jump yet one more wall. The horse failed. The Mad Marquess died, his neck broken in the crash.

Until the moment of Lord Henry's death, Delaval's father, John, had been a rural Anglican dean, but the fatal fall propelled the cleric, as next in line, into possession of Curraghmore and the title of fourth marquess of Waterford. Seven years later he, too, died, bringing his eldest son to the fore as the fifth marquess.

Delaval was the youngest of Lord John's five sons, fourteen years years behind the next youngest. He was probably spoiled rotten. At least, he was everybody's pet lamb as he toddled around a household full of his elders. But he was a lordly lamb. Unlike families with mere baronetcies, where only the eldest son inherited the title, every son of a marquess was a lord from the moment of his birth.

Delaval was still a boy when his father died and had special reason to mourn. Ancient custom dictated that, when Delaval's oldest brother succeeded to the title, his family moved to Curraghmore and the widow of the previous lord had to vacate the premises and move to a dower house. Delaval's mother left so her daughter-in-law could take charge of the mansion.

Lord Delaval James Beresford, youngest son of a distinguised Irish family, who ranched in Mexico. His death caused a sensation when his will revealed his gift of 10,000 dollars to his common-law wife, a black woman—a relationship illegal under Texas law where his will was probated. (From Lord Beresford and Lady Flo, Southwestern Studies No. 25 *by Eugene Porter. Photo courtesy of Texas Western Press, the University of Texas at El Paso.)*

Delaval occasionally visited his mother, but mostly he continued to live at Curraghmore. Here were the seeds to produce a classic remittance man. Lonely, stricken by the loss of his father and separation from his mother, he often cried himself to sleep. His Marquess brother, eighteen years his senior, treated him like a son. His sister-in-law, Lady Blanche, tried to comfort him, assuming a motherly role. But he remained in isolation, perhaps unable to forget that Lady Blanche was the reason his mother had left.

So Lord Delaval was a lonely, spoiled youth. Part of his restlessness may have echoed the Fenian Unrest, an independence movement that savagely harassed the landed Anglo-Irish families. To the north, in County Mayo, an estate manager, Captain Charles Boycott, was subjected to passive resistance from his tenants, giving rise to the descriptive word "boycott." But there was much violence, too. Anglo-Irish landlords were shot from hedgerows; families moved upstairs because snipers had greater difficulty targeting through upper windows. Loyal servants were beaten and dead animals often were thrown in wells. The Beresfords lost their foxhounds to poisoners and moved to Britain for several years until the bitterness abated.

Other factors helped create remittance men, however. Delaval's brothers were all embarked on what would be splendid careers—the marquess to run the estate, Lord Charles to become an admiral commanding Britain's Mediterranean Fleet, Lord William to win the Victoria Cross in the Zulu Wars in southern Africa and Lord Marcus to manage the Sandringham Stud (horse farm) for King Edward VII. Lord Delaval was probably overwhelmed by his brothers' prospects and achievements but saw little that interested him within their worlds.

It may have been the telling heritage of the Mad Marquess or an unhappy love affair, but by the time he was twenty-one Delaval was adventuring in the new world.

He may have visited Cuba. But one thing is certain: He soon was in Mexico, because the Mexican government in 1878 had fixed the price of public land at dirt cheap prices, as low as 12 cents a hectare (2.5 acres) for grazing land along the U.S. border, and Beresford had cattle ranching in mind.

Lord Delaval first bought a 73,500-acre ranch near Villa Ahumada, directly south of El Paso, and then moved sixty miles to the west where, on September 5, 1884, bought another ranch, the 160,000 acres known as Los Ojitos. Some twenty miles west of the village of Janos and one hundred miles southwest of El Paso, Los Ojitos was to be his home and headquarters until he died.

Ojo means "eye" in Spanish, but it is also the name for a spring, a precious natural phenomenon in a dry area like Chihuahua. Los Ojitos thus means "Little Springs."

The site was a magnet for travelers because the grove of willows and cottonwoods nourished by the springs was visible for miles—a green oasis nestled against a small hill and beckoning invitingly across the flat, brushy landscape. Low, grid mountain ranges far to the west broke an otherwise monotonous scene.

But to Lord Delaval the site spelled opportunity. Rainfall was slight but gramma grass, which cured well on the stalk, gave good forage. He needed wells and windmills to make the grass available for grazing. Even so, an animal would do a lot of walking: It took eighty acres of grass to supply the needs of a cow and her calf. Delaval's total holdings gave him sufficient range to graze nearly five thousand head of cattle.

He soon became a well-known figure in El Paso, a boon drinking companion at the Coney Island Saloon and other haunts frequented by cattlemen.

What happened next in his personal life is a subject of much conjecture and revolved around two developments: He took a black woman as a common-law wife, and his drinking bouts reached scandalous proportions.

A niece of Delaval's, Lady Clodagh Anson, gives some insight. As a small child at Curraghmore she had known Delaval in his teens. When she married the wealthy Claud Anson and joined him on a cattle ranch at San Angelo, Texas, she naturally wrote to her Uncle Delaval at Los Ojitos, inviting him to visit.

In her memoirs, written years later, Lady Clodagh said she learned belatedly that Delaval was a drunk, harmless to others but masochistic in his abuse of the bottle. According to Lady Clodagh, "He used to go on a razzle, and though he started out three times to see us, he never turned up, because after his orgy in [a nearby town, perhaps Janos] he always forgot why he had come there and just went home again." She explained that an unhappy first love had made Delaval "go all to bits" and he never returned to Ireland: "Whenever I saw an awful-looking rough tramp riding up to the ranch I used to think to myself, 'I do hope this is not Uncle Delaval.' "

It was at Los Ojitos that Lord Delaval received a fateful letter from the girl back home, telling him she was marrying someone else. According to Lady Clodagh's story, Delaval plunged into deep despair.

It was in this same mid-1880s period that he struck up an acquaintance with a new drinking companion, Florida J. Wolfe—a fateful meeting that was to catapult Delaval out of the ranks of just another remittance man into notoriety on an international scale.

Florida Wolfe was not only attractive and well educated— she was black. And this was a time when blacks and whites didn't mix socially in the United States or Europe. It was unusual in Chihuahua, too. Even a hundred years later, Mexican ranchers in the area would say, "Oh, yes, he was the one married to the black woman." Across the border in Texas social mixing was forbidden by law. Delaval once was fined for merely having the woman he called Lady Flo in his carriage upon crossing the Rio Grande into El Paso. After that they crossed in separate conveyances. Social mixing of the races was abhorrent to white Texans.

How did they meet? One story is that she had been abandoned by her black army husband, a noncommissioned officer, and that she met Delaval while working as a waitress. Another version held that Delaval became desperately ill with a fever and Florida nursed him back to health. A third story is that she was working in the U.S. consulate in Chihuahua City when they met. About the only certainty is that the 1880 federal census records Florida J. Wolfe, thirteen, as living in Salem, Illinois, with her widowed mother, Nancy. But there the certainies about her early life end. Her relationship with Delaval is verified repeatedly in the accounts of visitors to the ranch. And Delaval's will, filed in El Paso, promised her 10,000 dollars upon his death.

One of the earliest recorded visitors to Los Ojitos was a U.S. Army officer, Lieutant Britton Davis, who led a force of Apache scouts across Chihuahua in 1885, hunting for Geronimo. Stopping at Los Ojitos, he noted in his diary that Delaval, "being a proper Irishman," poured several rounds of alcohol before serving lunch to Davis and his party. But Davis evidently saw nothing of Lady Flo. A Texan, he almost certainly would have recorded the presence of Beresford's black paramour had she been present.

Other visitors met her at the adobe hacienda, set in the trees, apart from other buildings. As a boy, Herman Lindauer visited Los Ojitos, accompanying his father on business. With its eighteen-inch-thick walls supporting heavy roof beams the house was thirty feet long and ten feet wide. It was a cozy place. Young Lindauer described the scene:

> I remember sitting there in the ranch house in the twilight with my father and Lord Beresford, when this tall and stately colored woman entered and Lord Beresford introduced her with all the English royalty flourishes as "Lady Flo Beresford." She came over and sat on his lap. He bounced her on his knee and patted her on the fanny. I don't think at the time I had ever seen a colored person and I remember not being able to take my eyes off her in wonderment.

Cattlemen from New Mexico who knew the pair had little respect for Delaval. Said Alfred O. Boyd, Delaval's foreman for several years:

> Lord Beresford knew nothing of ranching. He was a remittance man; he was a drunkard. He was undoubtedly well educated but academic learning is no substitute for experience ... when one is attempting to operate a ranch.

A 1930s Associated Press feature story disagreed, at least in part, with the derogatory stories about Delaval. He was, the story noted, "a hard-bitten Englishman and a shrewd *hacendado*. His better hobbies were good cattle, good grass and beautiful horses, and his weaknesses were 'Lady Flo' and hard liquor."

The cattlemen all liked Lady Flo and credited her with much of Delaval's ranching success. Boyd said things were better managed after Lady Flo's arrival at the ranch: "The cowhands got out in the morning and attended to things as they had never done before. For the first time since Beresford bought the place they really worked."

Lady Flo expected them to work. She is quoted telling Boyd that, "I want to run this place so that it is self-supporting. Then the money that comes from England can be used to buy more land." Delaval was getting his remittances.

The ranch prospered and Delaval in 1902 indeed purchased more land in Alberta, Canada, but in a most whimsical way. He met a brand inspector who said the Red Deer Valley near Medicine Hat, Alberta, had good grass. That was enough for Delaval's itchy feet and, leaving Flo to run Los Ojitos, he drove seventy head of saddle horses and a herd of Mexican cattle to the nearest railhead. He settled in Alberta near the small community of Brooks.

Delaval called his new property the Mexico Ranch. He soon had one thousand cattle grazing on the land and, unusual for Delaval, he hired a competent staff to run it for him. His foreman was a veteran cowman from Texas called "Happy Jack" Jackson. Jackson loved pranks almost as much as the wild lords of Waterford. One time, riding through the outskirts of Brooks with Delaval, Jackson whipped his lariat over an outdoor privy and pulled it over, leaving a Brooks resident fully visible, his pants down and angrily waving his fist as Delaval and Jackson rode happily out of town.

Lord Delaval may not have obtained a deed to the Mexico Ranch land. Once he was accosted by an irate neighbor demanding that he stop running his cattle on the neighbor's Canadian property. Delaval invited the man inside for a drink. Two days later the visitor left, staggeringly drunk, but agreeing boozily that Delaval might be entitled to some use of the land.

But the best thing about the ranch may have been the happy times he and Lady Flo spent there in a tastefully designed cabin maintained for their use. They felt free in the much more tolerant social atmosphere of Canada and were able to make friends among the staff. The employee called their accommodations the Blue Parlor because it had blue-patterned chinaware, but the most prominent item was a large carved mahogany and walnut bed that had been shipped from the East. The massively ornate bedstead seemed as exotic as their unconventional relationship. They made numerous visits to the Mexico Ranch during the four years prior to 1907.

In those times railroads meant everything to the settlers. Farming and ranching weren't profitable if you couldn't reach market by rail. And rail was the only means of swift travel. Ironically, it was rail travel that ended the Beresfords' happy times.

Their shared life came to a sudden end at 2:15 A.M. December 23, 1906, at the small farm town of Enderlin, in eastern North Dakota. Behind schedule on his cold and icy run from the prairies of Alberta to Minneapolis, the Soo Line engineer had advanced the steam throttle to high speed—a fateful, tragic decison. At Enderlin his passenger train smashed into a switch engine.

Among the eleven dead in the wreckage was Delaval Beresford, 44, who was returning to Mexico from his Canadian ranch. At Minneapolis he had planned to catch a southbound train to Los Ojitos.

The press latched onto the glamour of the story. At a time when the West was full of fake British aristocrats who let people assume they were "lords," the dead man at Enderlin was the real thing. "Delaval Beresford was a Real Lord," said a headline in an El Paso newspaper. The fact that his brother, Lord Charles Beresford, was a famous British admiral raised the level of interest several more notches.

As Delaval's body was sent home from the embalmers in Minneapolis, the telegraph lines were humming with the story. On Christmas Day, the *London Times* printed the story of the wreck under the headline "American Train Disaster." It was an even bigger story in El Paso with the disclosure that Lord Delaval had been living the life of a remittance man and had willed part of his estate to his black common-law wife.

Titillation now increased reader interest on both sides of the Atlantic. In an era when southern states like Texas banned racial cohabitation, the Beresfords' daring relationship amazed, dumbfounded and horrified many of the readers who followed Lady

Flo's attempts in an El Paso court to secure her common-law claim to Delaval's million-dollar estate.

On December 29 the *London Times* noted the further developments with the report that Delaval's will, made in 1896, "bequeaths the sum of 2,000 pounds to a negro woman who nursed Lord Delaval through an attack of yellow fever. ... " That sum in 1907 equaled 10,000 dollars, a nice fortune by Western standards.

Although Lady Flo received sympathetic treatment from the press, she failed to establish proof either of a Mexican marriage or a common-law marriage in Texas, where the will was filed. There couldn't have been a marriage under Texas law, anyway; such marriages were illegal.

Lady Flo, then nearing forty, spent many months in 1907 trying to get some share of the ranching properties. Admiral Charles Beresford visited El Paso in February 1907, and asked for a meeting with her. She refused but gave no reason. Her decision may have been unwise because the admiral was a worldy man of considerable grace and might have been inclined to be generous. Finally, the court won an admission from Lady Flo that there had been no marriage. She insisted, however, that they had lived as man and wife. She was fighting for large stakes. When Delaval's estate was examined it totaled 233,500 acres. There was also a house in El Paso which Lady Flo occupied. Lord Charles' lawyer refused to grant more than the 10,000 dollars as specified in his brother's will but he finally agreed to an additional 5,000 dollar sum and Lady Flo agreed to relinquish all other claims.

Lord Charles' visit, meanwhile, was good copy. Newspapers reported that he had successfully shot quail at Los Ojitos Ranch and that he'd gone on to California after hiring an experienced ranch manager, Robert Moss of Roswell, New Mexico, to run the property—an arrangement that continued until Los Ojitos was sold for 190,000 dollars in 1910.

On his way home Lord Charles told the *New York Times* that he had been in America "winding up the affairs" of his brother, Delaval, "who died recently. ... " No reference was made to Lady Flo beyond his eliptical statement that troubles with the will "have been adjudicated." On April 11, 1907, the

London Times reported the admiral's return home, with a daughter, on the S.S. *Teutonic.*

Lady Flo stubbornly lived out her life in the role as widow of a lord. She had the words "Lady Flo" impressed into a concrete block at the curb of a house she bought in El Paso on August 10, 1907. She was a good neighbor, spoke fluent Spanish and attended the Second Baptist Church. At church suppers she would buy leftover food and distribute it to the poor.

When she died of tuberculosis on May 19, 1913, the doctor who signed her death certificate listed her marital status as "widowed." That enabled her to carry to the grave her title as an Irish Lady and perhaps more important her claim to having been a good wife and companion to a man who needed her. The title did not extend to her gravestone.

There was another memorial of sorts—the Beresfords' carved hardwood bed that first was displayed in a museum at Medicine Hat and later was sent to the Glenbow Museum in Calgary, a tribute to the closeness of their relationship.

In Ireland the Beresfords carried on. They survived the troubles over Irish independence and continued to operate Curraghmore, although on a much smaller scale than in centuries past. The current marquess of Waterford, great-great nephew of Delaval Beresford, farms a few hundred acres himself with the help of his son. In an interview in 1991 he said the Beresfords were able to hold the land because they stayed on it: "The trouble that arose with other families was generally caused by the fact that they were absentee landlords and failed to look after their properties and dependents." Then he added reflectively, "Although it is a struggle, we are attempting to maintain Curraghmore for as long as possible despite the penalitive taxes and inheritance laws."

Meanwhile, life goes on in the gramma and greasewood plains of Chihuahua where Lord Delaval found a few years of happiness. It has become a place of refuge for many besides Lord Delaval and Lady Flo. Soon after Delaval arrived, Mormon colonies—seeking refuge from U.S. laws against polygamy—settled at Casas Grandes, some forty miles from Los Ojitos.

In the 1920s a colony of Mennonites arrived from the north, many of them fleeing military conscription in Canada. The

Mormons and Mennonites—speaking English and Low German respectively, as well as Spanish—have prospered and upgraded local wage scales by starting agricultural processing plants.

Mexican families like the Bustillos, who today own the large ranch that includes the Los Ojitos property, also have found refuge and quiet—a far cry from the savagery of the Mexican Revolution eighty years ago—in the raising of yearling calves for the U.S. beef market. They know little about Beresford except that he, like they, found a good home and a good life in running cattle in a semi-arid land. But they know exactly where the ruins of Lord Delaval's adobe ranch house still stand in the rare, remote grove of trees—all that's left of a strange Englishman who made life hard for himself and others but never lacked courage or loyalty.

The author at the ruins of Los Ojitos Ranch, Janos, Chihuahua, Mexico.

And Their Ghosts Came with Them

Ghosts and spirits haunt every proper British castle, and any book about migrating Britons wouldn't be complete without them—because their occult powers (if you are a believer) reach around the globe.

The Beresfords of Waterford long have known that Curraghmore, the family seat in southern Ireland, houses a mysterious presence. Ladies of the family for some two hundred years have claimed a sudden affliction of the wrist as a premonition of death. It is said such a seizure occurred on December 23, 1906, when Delaval Beresford died in a train wreck in North Dakota: The women of Curraghmore said they anticipated a death before the telegram arrived.

Similarly, a restless spirit haunts Cortachy Castle, home of the aristocratic Ogilvys. The legend springs from a tragic misunderstanding in 1640. During that strife-torn year a Cameron drummer was sent to warn the Ogilvys of an impending attack by the duke of Argyll. The Cameron clansman drummed as he came through the woods to give advance warning to Cortachy's defenders. But the Ogilvys misunderstood his mission and executed him, either by hanging or by fire. In the latter version, the Ogilvys deliberately left him on the roof of their burning castle when Argyll attacked; true to his mission he continued drumming until the flames consumed him.

Since then, Ogilvy deaths have been signaled by ghostly drumming in the halls of the castle north of Dundee. When the eighth earl of Airlie, head of the clan, died in Colorado in 1881 of typhoid, his wife claimed the ghostly drumming preceded word of her husband's death. She heard it again when her eldest son was killed in the Boer War.

Another ghost story springs from southern Colorado. A beautiful British girl, Nell Fry, was staying at a ranch near Pueblo in 1916–17. She was in love with a young British artist named Jack McKenzie, who had visited the area earlier but who had gone home to enlist for the war in France. Kay Jensen of Fowler, Colorado, takes up the story:

> Nell was staying at the Lees-Livesay Ranch in 1916 or 1917. One morning Nell got up and said to Jack Redmond, one of the ranch hands: "I was looking out the window last night and I saw Jack McKenzie riding by." Redmond responded: "Well, I heard hoofbeats myself last night." Of course, word soon came that McKenzie had been killed on the Western Front the night that Nell saw the ghostly rider.

Mrs. Jensen adds, "Why wouldn't he have come riding by? He loved this country."

Well, why not? Nell went back to England and never married. One wonders how many times she wakened at night to the memory of ghostly hoofbeats in the hills of far-off Colorado.

✤

CHAPTER 13

"Can a Girl
from a Mining Town ... ?"

"You in England are prisoned in pens," declared a young Ethel Barrymore, sweeping to center stage at Broadway's Hudson Theatre in November 1904. Addressing fellow actors playing her snobbish English in-laws in fictional Brinthrope Abbey, she accused them of regarding Americans as savages and then continued:

> You live in the past. We live in the future. You speak of home. Well, so do we. Out there where I came from [a California mining camp] there are homes that we love. They're not such mighty fixtures as Brinthrope Abbey but we love 'em just the same.

Ethel Barrymore, then twenty-five, was playing the title role of an orphan girl, Sunday, reared by four rough but kindly California miners. She meets Lord Henry Brinthrope, falls in love and is carried away to be lady of an English manor house, Brinthrope Abbey. Their true love runs anything but smoothly.

This play earned a footnote in theatrical history because of a single line. When Ethel finished her pretty soliloquy to her snooty in-laws, she added a wonderful and memorable bit of improvisation: "That's all there is; there isn't any more."

Although it lasted only briefly, the play, "Sunday," is nonetheless pivotal. It gave rise more than thirty years later to one of American radio's most popular soap operas, "Our Gal Sunday." In her 1937 radio debut, Sunday was from Colorado, not California, and Lord Henry now lived in Black Swan Hall in Virginia, but the plot was the same: poor Sunday suffered daily indignities from her lordly husband and his overbearing English friends. America's love-hate relationship with the British was tested to its limits.

With the lugubrious strains of "Red River Valley" groaning in the background, each day's episode was introduced with the same prelude as a story about "an orphan girl from the little mining town of Silver Creek, Colorado ... married to England's richest, most handsome lord—Lord Henry Brinthrope—the story that asks the question, can this girl from a mining town in the West find happiness as the wife of a wealthy and titled Englishman?"

A sympathetic American housewife, standing at her ironing board with her ear attuned to a nearby radio, could have savagely burned holes in a gross of shirts while she chafed at the dastardly abuse piled daily upon poor Sunday by her feckless mate week after week, year after year. "Our Gal Sunday" had its greatest audience in the Midwest, where isolationism was fed by anti-British sentiment. The drama was finally canceled in 1959 after an incredibly durable twenty-two-year run.

The drama is important, too, because it had the temerity to deal not only with a cross-Atlantic love affair but an upper class–lower class one at that. It conveyed quite casually a grand spoof of foppish British gentlemen depending for strength on the sturdy, common-sense women of America. But it also reflected the depth to which British culture continued to flourish even after emigrants from the European continent far surpassed Britain as a source of the new Americans. British values were strong and so was the appetite for news stories of scandal and human interest generated in Britain.

In part, the 1904 play drew on real life. Americans were well aware of the decadence and hypocrisy of British culture late in the nineteenth century. They knew about the hundreds of impoverished young British aristocrats who sought—often quite brazenly—to "buy" brides in America. Their search was not for middle class girls like Sunday but heiresses. Any American millionaire willing to put up a few hundred thousand dollars as dowry could marry his daughter into a title and see her ladyship become mistress of an ancient manor house, possibly a great estate like Blenheim Castle. This castle fell to Consuelo Vanderbilt who, in the 1880s, married the ninth duke of Marlborough and brought with her a immense dowry: U.S. railroad stock worth 4.2 million dollars. The magnificent castle was extensively rebuilt thanks to American resources.

Except for the large sums involved, the heiress trade sank almost to the level of a colonial slave market. In one case, a man describing himself as a "a peer of very old title" advertised in the *Daily Telegraph* for a "very wealthy lady." His targets were the London representatives of wealthy American families. He came right to the point: "If among your clients you know such a lady, who is willing to purchase the rank of a peeress for 65,000 pounds sterling, paid in cash, and who has sufficient wealth besides to keep up the rank of peeress, I should be pleased if you would communicate with me."

While his father didn't advertise, no less a figure than Winston Churchill was the offspring of such a marriage. His mother was Jennie Jerome, daughter of a millionaire New York investor and publisher (for a short time he was a major shareholder in the *New York Times*). Winston's father, Lord Randolph Churchill—like so many other hard-up second sons—needed money to stay in politics and Jennie's father, Leonard Jerome, had it.

Class distinctions might be anathema to middle and lower class Americans—and American males might hoot at the hypocrisy of monocled English gentlemen combing the colonies for heiresses—but many an American girl let her mind wander: Wouldn't it be romantic to be married to a literate, sophisticated Englishman, supervising a mansion full of servants? The suave, impeccably dressed Englishman became a stock fantasy figure.

So Sunday and her Lord Brinthrope bestrode the American stage and airwaves. But about this drama is a nearly incredible coincidence. Fantastic as the plot might seem, a flesh-and-blood marriage in Colorado endured the same theme at virtually the same time. This marriage of unlikely partners was being battled through in Colorado and Great Britain by Sir Cecil and Lady Moon. The difference was that the pristine character projected by Sunday could not begin to describe Lady Moon. Unlike long-suffering Sunday, Lady Moon was an immigrant Irish washerwoman who took the fight to her wimpish, boozing, cricket-playing husband. She was poor but she wore the pants. In fact, Lady Moon seems to have delved into Sir Cecil's inheritance sufficiently to help grease the skids to the ultimate bankruptcy he no doubt deserved.

Cecil Moon was from Liverpool, one of the hundreds of adventuring young Britons attracted to the West's mines and cattle ranges in the nineteenth century. They brought millions of pounds of British sterling with them in search of opportunity and fun—not necessarily in that order.

Still in his teens, Cecil landed in Georgetown, Colorado, to work as an accountant at a silver mine high on Argentine Pass. His family was paying the expenses to give him the experience and responsibility he would need as a future baronet and heir to the family's industrial wealth. What they got, instead, was a remittance man and wastrel.

Cecil's grandfather, Sir Richard Moon, was the man who had put the Moons on the map—and in *Burke's Peerage*. Born in 1814, Richard Moon became famous as the industrialist who built the London and North Western Railway into one of the most powerful institutions in Britain. So notable were his achievements that Queen Victoria knighted him in 1887.

Cecil, born in 1867, could expect to progress in leisurely fashion to the title of third baronet in mid-life, after his father's death. But his father died early, before his grandfather, who died in 1899. In that year, then, Sir Cecil Moon at 32, was the youthful second baronet with easy access to the inheritance.

But that's getting ahead of the story. Working for the silver mine in 1885 proved a disaster. Cecil may have found life high above timberline boring. Or he may have spent too much time watching the soaring birds of prey, the "whistle pigs" (marmots) and other sights that made the surrounding tundra more interest-ing than mining. In any case, he soon was reduced to working as an outdoor manual laborer on a mine tunnel project at 2.50 dollars per day.

Newspaper records show that Cecil had moved to the low foothills near Fort Collins, Colorado, to do what many British remittance men did in those days—study to be a cattle rancher. His remittance from home covered the tuition.

The "cow school" was near another mining camp called Manhattan—today one of the hundreds of long-forgotten Western settlements where miners rushed to new diggings only to discover that the deposits of precious metals were not economical. Manhattan rose quickly to a peak population of two hundred, then dwindled and within a half century was gone—not even a ghost town. But while the fling lasted Manhattan produced something that changed Cecil Moon's life forever—a buxom Irish-American girl named Katie Lawder.

Cecil was lodged a short distance from Manhattan at a school operated by a retired British army man, Captain Roxby. In the wake of the cattle boom of the 1870s, Britons invested heavily in Western cattle ranching. Realizing that young British gentlemen were in surplus, people like Captain Roxby advertised their services in British publications: For a few hundred pounds they would turn any polite, soft-handed, cricket-playing British schoolboy into a self-sufficient cattle rancher.

Captain Roxby had a beautiful ranch called Ashley Grange. His tuition ranged from 300 to 500 dollars a year, but apparently his instruction was excellent—several of his trainees settled nearby as successful ranchers. But Cecil Moon, if not a brilliant student, had something even better—enough cash to buy out the teacher.

Roxby, who was following a pattern common through the United States and Canada, had made money schooling gentlemen ranchers. But selling out was even better. So the other pupils—nicknamed "pups"—were turned out and Cecil Moon took over the ranch.

Whether Cecil would have become a capable and resourceful rancher on his own will never be known—because of his marriage to Katie Lawder, which came about in the following manner.

Having been sent as a child to the United States, Katie had grown up in Clinton, Iowa, working as a servant girl. In her teens she set out to seek her fortune, and fate put her in the Manhattan mining camp. There she took in washing as wife (perhaps in common-law status) to a dollar-a-day miner, Frank Gartman.

Lady Moon, Irish washerwoman, who married a wimpish British baronet, Sir Cecil Moon. The pair separated after she scandalized his English relatives by riding dressed in pants and cowboy boots, to the hounds on a Colorado quarter horse. (Photo courtesy of the Denver Public Library, Western History Department.)

One day she was called to Ashley Grange to nurse young Moon during an illness. Being a washerwoman, she had ample access to community gossip and was quite aware of Cecil's excellent prospects. She put her earthy charms to work and soon won the day. Love replaced illness and Katie sent her miner husband packing so she could marry young Cecil. That was in 1888. If Katie was a hard-eyed adventuress, so be it. Maybe Cecil needed a rough-minded wife to manage his life for him. At eighteen, she was a good deal more mature than Cecil was at twenty-one.

Recognizing their future heir's marital obligations, the Moon family in Britain gave Cecil considerable financial help to establish himself as a rancher—even before his elevation to the peerage in 1899. With his various windfalls, Moon acquired not only Ashley Grange but other land besides. Katie pitched in with vigor and soon was driving cattle on the range. She also discovered that a washerwoman's language was easily understood—and even appreciated—by the cowboys.

The marriage at first was, by turns, happy and chaotic. One story persists that Cecil's aristocratic mother made the then-arduous trip to America to see her new daughter-in-law and, after one horrified look, summoned a Boston dressmaker by train to Colorado to try to put a veneer of culture on Lady Moon. But the rags-to-gentility theme was to have no parallel here. Katie Moon dressed and talked like a washerwoman because that's what she was. The effort collapsed. No Liza Doolittle future for her.

Sir Cecil and Lady Moon made their own good times, however. They lived in a log ranch house, drank good whiskey, read English books and papers and helped herd the cattle, with "cow servants" doing the heavy work. They had a butler sent lock, stock and accent from England. Cecil loved to play cricket and joined a Denver team for organized regional matches.

A few years later the marriage was in shreds when Lady Moon joined her husband on a trip to Britain to claim his title. As a baronet, Cecil now had social duties at home and made several trips home. But Lady Moon's coarse manners scandalized her in-laws. Her riding ability was excellent and she brought her own Colorado quarter horse, Mose, across the Atlantic for fox hunts. But there was no scarlet tunic for her fox hunts. She dressed just as she would for a roundup, with rough clothing and boots. And one may assume that "tally-ho" and "yoicks" gave way to, "There goes the little bugger" and "Come on, you lazy hounds." At least in Colorado—and perhaps Britain, too—she had a blunt habit of generically addressing people as "Buster."

The upscale Moon in-laws were aghast and soon began disinviting her to family functions, even if she was by title a lady. Sometimes they held functions on the sly. When it was time to return to the American West the pair detoured by way of Paris, where Sir Cecil lost thousands of dollars gambling. Years later Sir Cecil showed his Colorado friends a framed canceled check for 10,000 dollars that he said was a gambling debt.

Could the Moons have inspired the 1904 play, "Sunday?" It's unlikely because their headline-grabbing marital fireworks occurred later, in 1909, when Sir Cecil sued his wife for divorce and asked the return of 61,000 dollars in securities he claimed she had misappropriated. By then the play was history.

What really gave the Moons a field day in the Denver newspapers was Sir Cecil's claim in court filings that his wife forced him to do dishes and generally bossed him unmercifully. A lord doing dishes? Cartoonists loved it. Lady Moon responded that somebody had to boss the weakling. She then gratuitously dragged out some dirty linen, alleging that Sir Cecil had been fired from his mining jobs in the 1880s for incompetence. "I owe him nothing," she told the court. She was awarded 2,250 dollars and some of the land.

Katie lost her title in the court settlement, but her neighbors continued to call her Lady Moon as a courtesy. She kept on ranching, making life miserable for neighboring ranchers, who complained that she turned her uncastrated bull calves onto the common range, thus making a mockery of efforts to upgrade the stock through selective breeding.

She also was accused of selling home-distilled whiskey during Prohibition. At one point, revenue officers found her with bottles of illegal whiskey tied to the corset under her dress. She claimed she was just being sociable and that neighboring ranchers rather appreciated her efforts.

Although she tried to correct her speech, grammar remained beyond the pale. Once, while she was using her best conversational abilities for the benefit of a visiting church pastor, she uncovered the cage of her pet parrot. The bird immediately assailed the pastor with language blue enough to shame a seasoned cowboy.

When she died in 1926 she was given fulsome newspaper tributes that reported sympathetically that she had wanted "Lady Moon" inscribed on her tombstone. Her request was refused and the headstone of her grave in a Catholic cemetery near Denver to this day merely says "Moon."

After the divorce Sir Cecil went back to Britain and in 1912 remarried—this time to Lillian Mary Preston, daughter of a cleric and widow of a physician. The couple settled into quiet country life. On October 17 of that year the *London Times* recorded his bankruptcy in the Tunbridge Wells County Court. It showed that on his return to Britain in 1909 he had only 65 pounds and numerous liabilities. The court noted that he held thousands of shares in Colorado mining and transportation companies, and that he had been a director of some of them. But as the court then noted, "The debtor attributes his present position to failure of companies in which he was interested and inability to obtain remunerative employment."

Sir Cecil outlived Katie by twenty-five years, dying in Buxton on February 22, 1951. The baronetcy went to his cousin, Richard Moon, then fifty years old.

The Moons' story holds uncanny symbolism for the whole period when remittance men adventured west for excitement and opportunity. The crash of the Moons' marriage—the triumph of reality over romantic impulse—reflected the strains in the Anglo-American relationship. The only thing worse than being divided by a common language was the joining in marriage of two people with as many weaknesses as this strange combination of tough washerwoman and gentleman wimp.

But it may have been a more common story than appears in historical records. The frontier wasn't a place where young Englishmen, remittance men or otherwise, were likely to find a great variety of choice in the women they met. A Briton—long resident of Colorado—made his own observations: "There weren't many women on the frontier and those that were here were diamonds in the rough—very rough." Americans, of course, countered that many Englishmen on the frontier, especially remittance men, were so helpless they needed nursemaids. Like the American cowboy who projected a romantic image but wasn't notable as marital timber, the symbolic English adventurer couldn't stand close examination, either.

Writers at the turn of the century knew the theme very well. The "Sunday" script as played by Ethel Barrymore was done by three English actors whose names were jumbled into the pen name Thomas Raceward, making their identities doubtful. But other authors like Hamlin Garland, a Pulitzer Prize winner in 1921, and James Michener, in *Tales of the South Pacific*, used the remittance man to good effect.

Americans have been more sympathetic than Australians, who regarded the remittance man as a drifter of little consequence. Canadians understood him but made him the butt of innumerable jokes. Sir Cecil Moon fell into the latter category, finding himself lampooned in a Denver cartoon with monocle and mustache while doing the kitchen dishes.

Many a younger son discovered that his family's overseas arrangements for him were mainly to tidy up the debris left by primogeniture and that receiving remittances in some godforsaken wilderness was worse than charity. He was often victimized by ranch school promoters far worse than Captain Roxby. As fellow Britons, they easily won his confidence.

But the family didn't seem to care as long as the younger son was out of sight. No wonder the remittance man often took to drink and saw no reason to complicate matters further by getting married. Cecil Moon, on the other hand, took the gamble and learned through bitter experience that frontier marriages were chancy affairs. Probably a majority of British gentlemen migrants remained single.

I'm in for a Title or Something

There came to the ranch house on foot a tall, dusty Englishman, under his arm a little sewing machine. He asked for work.

"Ranch work?" asked the owner.

"No," said the Englishman. "I'm rather tired of that. Sewing is what I want. I'm rather good at sewing. I'll keep all your clothes, and saddles and things, and everybody else's in order."

And he did [but] at the end of five years he turned up for supper one night and said, "Sorry! I got a letter this afternoon and I'm afraid I'll have to be going. My father's dead, and I suppose I'm in for a title or something."

—*Struthers Burt*
Powder River, Let'er Buck

❧

CHAPTER 14

The Cowboy Baronet

The world in 1882 was a wonderful place for an Englishman bent on travel and adventure. The British flag snapped in friendly breezes—both frigid and tropical—on six continents. If you were a well-heeled British schoolboy intent on going to sea, punching cows in the Wild West or shooting tigers in the Far East—well, why not?

But at age thirteen? Victorian sons, of course, left home early for boarding school—but seldom to see the world at thirteen. Yet that was the decision a rebellious Leicestershire lad arrived at in 1882. He remained abroad nearly four decades. He fought several wars, shot twenty-nine tigers and branded cattle in the American West—an aristocratic cowboy proud of his toughened, rope-burned hands.

This almost unbelievable tale centers around Sir Genille Cave-Browne-Cave, twelfth baronet of Stretton Hall at Stretton-en-le-Field in the English Midlands. He was born there September 3, 1869, to Sir Mylles and Lady Isabelle Cave-Browne-Cave, whose titles and land claims dated from the Norman Conquest. Genille was their second son but after his older brother, Geoffry, died in 1880, Genille became—at age eleven—heir apparent to one of the oldest titles in England.

181

No matter how hard the family tried to educate Genille through tutoring and by enrolling him at Repton, a highly regarded public school, he floundered. He said later that books were "my pet abomination unless they happened to be stories of adventure or had anything to do with the sea."

So like hundreds of other young English gentlemen—including Winston Churchill—he came to detest the repressive atmosphere of the public school.

The future twelfth baronet became a misfit. His father hired tutor after tutor but the boy only fought harder, on one occasion calling a German governess a fool, which earned him a thrashing. He ran away from home but was captured and thrashed again. Locked in his room, he picked the lock and earned yet another thrashing. But he finally made his escape and joined a circus.

He performed as a juvenile rider in the circus's steeplechase act, teamed with a girl his age. When his family came searching for him, Genille and the girl switched costumes and he escaped detection. Finally hunted down, Genille so stubbornly rejected his father's plans that at last he was indentured as an apprentice on a sailing ship plying the Australian trade route. It was the life he wanted. "That call of the wild that has never left me," he wrote later in his memoirs.

So just short of fourteen, he boarded a tall-masted sailing ship and began abruptly to learn about the world. Early in the voyage he addressed a black crew member as "Sambo" and was, he said, "felled by a tremendous crack on the head." Regaining his senses he was told the man's proper name was "Doctah," an instruction young Genille quickly took to heart. Apprentices were forbidden to smoke or drink but the captain profiteered by selling both products at a handsome markup to crewmen regardless of age. Young Genille got the adventure he sought when the ship sailed into a sudden, savage hurricane one night. The captain on deck shouted hasty commands to the crew high overhead, fighting desperately to shorten sail before the screaming winds swamped the vessel. Although Genille and his mates, clinging precariously to the swaying yardarms, could see nothing in the inky blackness they reefed in the canvas and saved the ship.

Genille quickly grew in height and strength as sea duty took him to most of the world's great ports. Although his indenture was for four years, he and a companion jumped ship in Australia and got jobs clearing land and fighting the rabbit plague. Next, he wandered through the Outback. At one station young Cave (he shortened his name overseas) learned a new dimension of the word, "Sundowner." Arriving at the station at sunset, he asked for a night's lodging but found the rancher nervous and reticent. When Genille offered to trade tobacco for a meal and lodging, the rancher's demeanor brightened and he confessed that he had mistaken the youth for a Sundowner: "A class of man little better than a tramp, who, if the settlers will not give him shelter and food, has a nasty habit of firing the premises ... ."

One other nastiness Genille observed in Australia was a sea captain's vicious practice—when he needed sailors—of sending ashore for a parson to "minister to a dying sailor." Once aboard, the pastor was clubbed and impressed into the crew.

Genille arrived home in England in 1885 and enlisted in a cavalry regiment. But he soon faced imprisonment for dereliction of duty. Only through his father's intervention did he escape punishment to sail with his unit for peacetime service in India. Finding a colonial soldier's life intolerably dull, bearable only through recourse to liquor, he volunteered for an Afghan expedition but found that dull, too. He resigned the cavalry and tried his hand at gold mining in the South Indian state of Mysore. But once he had earned 3,000 rupees he set out for Burma and joined a police unit fighting a fierce war with Dacoits, a murderous caste. He barely escaped with his life in a no-quarter pistol-and-sword fight in which Genille's small police force surprised the Dacoits inside their fortress at night and slew three hundred of them. He later served in the Spanish-American War and the Boxer Rebellion.

At this stage of his life Genille was receiving ample remittances from home. Although reluctant to detail his finances, he admitted later that he had purchased his way out of the cavalry in India for "several hundred rupees," adding: "I always had an allowance from home and the money part of it didn't bother."

That was about to change. Back home, he found that his father, Sir Mylles, was spending money as fast as he was. Since his title to the estate was entailed (guaranteed by law), Genille borrowed up to the equivalent of 55,000 dollars in loans against Stretton Hall. He spent it in three months. Next, he bounced off briefly on safari in Africa, then to Burma, where he became a tiger bounty hunter. He claimed he killed twenty-nine tigers and, besides bounty money, earned plenty of excitement; his hunting partner was killed by a tiger.

But his profligate borrowing now produced dire consequences in Britain. Genille said: "The money lenders went up to see my father's attorneys. Then there was a fine row and I never saw the guv'nor again. He cast me off. I never had another communication from him." From that moment on Genille earned his passage.

Still in his 20s, he joined the crew of a vessel bound for Greenland where he spent some weeks studying Eskimo culture. But recalling the thrill of seeing a Wild West show in London, he resolved to experience the real thing in the American West. So he sailed to the East Coast of the United States. He worked his way west, bribing conductors to let him ride in empty boxcars. From Kansas City he journeyed to western Kansas and was hired by a rancher. As a newcomer he was given a vicious bronco on his first day as a ranch hand. He landed hard but kept trying and soon mastered broncobusting. A Texan taught him the use of a six-gun and he claimed he became expert enough to shoot the revolver from the hand of an outlaw. A bit far-fetched!

Next, he found jobs in Colorado, Wyoming and Utah. His personal narrative—*From Cowboy to Pulpit*—written later in life reported bitter experiences among the Mormons. He recited Mormon atrocities, claiming that gentile ranchers were slain by Mormon raiders intent on kidnapping their daughters for bigamous marriages. He was dismissed from a job for being non-Mormon.

In Wyoming, thirty miles out of Cheyenne, he worked for a rancher he called "mean as a snake." That conclusion came from his boss's treatment of a cowgirl given work on the ranch. Genille declared that cowpunching was "too rough for women" and was outraged when the rancher gave the girl a day's work and had her cook dinner. Then, well after dark, he told her to get her pony and leave—without pay—assuring her that the next ranch was "only eighteen miles away." Genille's strong language may explain his sparing use of names, places and dates.

Genille's Colorado experiences are tantalizing. He mentions being in Denver, Pueblo and Montrose but gives few names. At Montrose, he ran afoul of the law several times. On one occasion he and some other cowboys made a nighttime raid on a ranch in Paradise Valley, inserting long, supporting poles under a Scotsman's henhouse and carrying off the entire structure. Reaching a safe distance they killed the squawking chickens for food.

The irate Scotsman filed charges but Genille and his friends proved in court—with the help of friendly witnesses—that they were nowhere near Paradise Valley when the thievery took place. In his book, Genille admits his guilt. There is a Paradox Valley west of Montrose: Could this be the place, disguised, that Genille wrote about?

Colorado justice was usually casual. One judge had Genille arrested and brought to the bench where he levied a trumped-up fine of 10 dollars. When Genille protested the justice said, "Now, look here, I wouldn't have fined you, but I was almighty dry, and I hadn't got a damned cent, so I had to send the sheriff out to find somebody, and he came across you. Come on, let's spend it." They did—at the nearest bar.

Genille also worked briefly in Arizona, Texas and Louisiana. In the latter state he added to his professional repertory by hiring out as a lumberjack felling cypress trees in a swamp. Often penniless, he never shunned work and would accept such dirty jobs as cleaning out cattle cars and digging ditches.

In 1908, Genille became an international celebrity. His father's death on January 22, 1907, lifted him to the peerage. But where was he? Nearly a year later the discovery that young Cave—now Sir Genille—was working in Colorado as a cowboy brought wide press attention.

In a rambling story on January 5, 1908, the *Denver Republican* reported that Genille had recently engaged in a "wordy quarrel" with a western Colorado rancher named M. L. English and had been fined. Rather than pay up, Genille left Montrose to work as a day laborer in Utah.

The *Republican*'s informant evidently was Frank Prestidge, a Denver attorney and a friend of Genille's. In *From Cowboy to Pulpit*, Genille relates being a guest at the residence of "a Denver attorney"—probably Prestidge—when a rural sheriff came to the door to arrest him. Genille overheard the conversation and realized that he and the sheriff had never met. So he quickly told his host to invite the sheriff to dinner and that Genille would pretend to be the butler. The ruse worked perfectly and the well-fed sheriff departed happily but without his prisoner.

Did it really happen? Genille claims it did.

The main interest of Denver journalists was in Genille's future peerage plans. Reporters assumed that, as in the fairytale, the ugly duckling now would sail home to claim the wealth of Stretton Hall. They guessed wrong. Sir Genille had no specific plans, other than to indulge in a bit of whimsy with a reporter from *The Denver Post* in a story printed February 13, 1908:

> Why, over there I'll be a justice of the peace and deputy lord lieutenant of the county. Can you see me sitting up there? I'd be a nice fellow to bring a poacher before, wouldn't I? —Me that's stolen as many calves as I have, judging a man for stealing a pair of rabbits!

But Sir Genille's homecoming was anything but triumphal, nor were there trumpet flourishes at Stretton Hall. The free-spending Sir Mylles had left a legacy of disaster—a debt of 64,000 pounds, more than half the estate's value of 100,000 pounds.

Sir Genille summed up his trip home in one paragraph:

> I soon found out that the family estates at Stretton were in a very bad way. I went over them and also over my old home, and, astounded, I had no idea that things were going as bad as they were. I soon came to the conclusion that the best thing to do was to sell out, lock, stock and barrel.

He gave the proceeds, less than 2,000 pounds, to the church. The exact date of this event is uncertain, but it predated 1910.

The family was not happy. In a letter to Prestidge in Denver, Genille's mother, Lady Isabelle, now living elsewhere in Britain, washed her hands of the whole affair, declaring, "Genille has chosen his life; let him abide by it."

Other stories took a different tack. R. C. Cave-Browne-Cave, an admiral in the British Navy, wrote to Prestidge suggesting that his kin, Sir Genille, might marry a wealthy American girl and return to England with enough money to keep the estate in the family. He hoped Prestidge might help find a Denver girl with sufficient dowry to exchange a trip to the altar for an ancient and noble title. For a time the prospect seemed a lively one.

The Denver Post pursued this theme throughout 1908. One story said Sir Genille would marry a wealthy Denver girl, Miss E. Chancellor, but it soon was retracted. A Miss Browning was next on the *Post's* matrimonial list, but that story put egg on the *Post's* face when a Denver bank clerk announced that he, not Sir Genille, was going to marry the girl.

By 1908, pledging a lustrous British title in a nuptial deal with a moneyed American girl was commonplace, and Sir Genille said he almost succumbed. After moving to New York he was contacted by a lawyer who asked if he wanted to get married. "Damned if I know," said Genille, whereupon the lawyer said: "I've got a girl with five million dollars—I'll pay all your family debts and give you a quarter million for yourself. You marry her and take her into English Society." Sir Genille agreed reluctantly to go to Washington where the girl was staying at a fashionable hotel with her secretary. He arrived at the hotel, sent up his card and soon heard the same offer from the secretary. But as he awaited the arrival of the girl he got angry.

"What a beastly business," he wrote. "What a cad I should be to even see the girl ... being forced to marry like this by relatives. So, writing a note on a piece of hotel notepaper—'Sorry I can't wait'—I slipped out of the hotel ... taking the first train back to New York."

After seeing the lawyer, Genille said, "I expect he thought I was worse than mad for not marrying the girl and letting him make a good fat fee."

Genille spent the next decade in the eastern United States, working for a time as a movie double in scenes requiring riding and roping. Then a strange thing happened: He got religion in a barroom. While he was drinking with his friends, a Salvation Army lassie entered looking for contributions and when she asked him to attend an open-air gospel meeting, he promised he would, to which his drinking companions shouted, "Go it, you mad devil. ... Hell will be turned loose now."

But Genille went and was converted to a fare-thee-well. Through the Salvation Army, he secured a post as a pulpit-pounding preacher. His longest tour of duty was two years spent among backwoods families in Virginia, where even this one-time hobo was shocked by the poverty of his congregation. On one occasion he killed and butchered a hog for an elderly lady.

In World War I Genille crossed north into Canada and enlisted. He soon was in Britain drilling recruits as a Canadian Army corporal. But religion prevailed and he soon was reassigned to duties as a chaplain. When he was demobilized, a benefactor, whom he identifies in his book only as a relative, paid his tuition for a year's training at London Theological College. He took orders in the Church of England in 1920. Thus prepared and ordained, he first became a deacon in a large church of sixteen thousand members and finally won appointment to a country parish at Londesborough in Yorkshire. In 1926, he married the daughter of a churchwarden, Mary Elizabeth Wreghitt. The marriage endured until Sir Genille's death in 1929. His title passed to a cousin.

There have been four other baronets in the Cave-Browne-Cave line since Sir Genille. The current baronet is the sixteenth, Sir Robert Cave-Browne-Cave, born in 1929, and a resident of Vancouver, British Columbia. He heads the family genealogical society, which has recorded fifteen thousand Cave-Browne-Cave descendants scattered around the world.

In an interview, Sir Robert was philosophical about the twelfth baronet's adventuresome life. Of the church assignment he says, "I think his living (stipend at the parish) was purchased for him," perhaps by the same relative who financed his theological degree.

But other family members were aghast at the rector's western slang which, according to Sir Robert, often went like this: "And there I was a-ridin' my hoss down this little dry arroyo with my Colt six-gun at the ready ... . "

Not exactly high church. His gun-fighting imagery in his sermons and his posturing as a fugitive from American justice shamed his upper class relatives so deeply that, when his autobiography appeared, they bought up and sequestered as many copies of it as they could, thus explaining the scarcity of the book today.

Of the family finances, Sir Robert said:

> [Genille's] father was quite a spendthrift and the old house at Stretton Hall went for mortgages before the First War ... between them they squandered whatever money there was. His father, I believe, is the one who largely squandered it. But Genille probably had his share of it.

Stretton Hall, built in 1350 and rebuilt in 1750, has been replaced and is no longer occupied by Cave-Browne-Cave descendants. However, Sir Robert added, "There's a fellow in England who claims that I own the family home but I'm staying out of that one."

On January 17, 1992, Sir Robert wrote about the research on this book, stating,

> I ask you not to be too hard on my great-great uncle or whatever, but I do hope this will help you in your research. Ah! the "Wild West." Was it as Hollywood made it? Or was it just a bunch of adventurous Easterners trying to make a decent living along with the usual group of "con artists" and "bad types"?

He put down Genille's autobiography as "part fiction and part truth," concluding that "even the old colonials had some fun." But Sir Robert is long past worrying about publicity adverse to an old and noble family. His letter explained, "If you are a student of P. G. Wodehouse, you may remember a paragraph in *Carry on Jeeves,* the first of the books about Bertie Wooster:

> I think you overestimate the danger of people being offended by being in these recollections. It has been my experience, Sir, that the normal person enjoys seeing his or her name in print,

irrespective of what is said about them ... Moreover, if you have studied psychology, Sir, you will know that respectable old gentlemen are by no means averse to having it advertised that they were extremely wild in their youth ... .

So on with the game of rattling family skeletons, although Sir Robert still expresses exasperation over the fact that Sir Genille, in his zealous conversion to Christianity, willed away the family silver to the Anglican Church. "It took us years to buy it back," he says ruefully.

Despite his wanderings, Sir Genille Cave-Browne-Cave earned respect. On October 30, 1929, his obituary in the *London Times*, ran nearly half a column and an editorial paid tribute to his "varied and adventurous career." In sixty years he was many things, often deeply contradictory, but he never lacked courage or denied friendly help to others when manly principles were at stake.

✤
_____

British Snobbery: How Bad?

By today's standards British snobbery was brutal, according to John L. Sinclair, eighty-nine, a New Mexico cowboy and archeologist. Now living at Bernalillo, New Mexico, Sinclair described his upper middle class boyhood in Scotland:

> My family—originally named St. Clair before they crossed the channel from Normandy in 1066—was in weaving. They made tartans and, later, marketed tweeds handwoven in the Hebrides. We had eight servants but I couldn't talk to them. They were beneath me. Eating fish and chips also was forbidden as "vulgar." You didn't read Robert Burns' poetry, because he was a common ploughman. And if a young gentleman did break the rules and make a pass at a serving girl she had no recourse.

When Sinclair's father—who became a sea captain—married a plain Australian girl, the family's ostracism was so ugly that it may have contributed to her early death. Later assigned as a shipping company official in New York City, the father (also named John) swore he would never tell his family when he remarried to an Irish immigrant girl.

"He never did, either," says Sinclair. "When he died in 1906 my mother had to tell them about the marriage—and about me. My grandfather sent me to Perse School, an exclusive academy at Cambridge. I spent four years there but I didn't like it; I wanted farming and livestock."

The curse of gentility now reared its head. The family offered to help Sinclair become a gentleman fruit farmer in western Canada and he actually boarded a ship with that intent. But he toured the United States on the way:

When I saw New Mexico I knew I wanted to be a cowboy. But that was beneath them, too, so they told me my ranching career would be without their blessing—and that was all right with me. I became a cowboy and finally an archeologist for the state—and that's what I've done ever since. I've never regretted it.

Sinclair first heard the term "remittance man," in Santa Fe in the 1920s. While he isn't a classic remitter (his family wasn't ousting him), he received semiannual interest payments from his grandfather's estate for some years. But, he added, "I must admit I come from a class that produced a lot of them."

✤

CHAPTER 15

Problems They Didn't Talk About

Historically, the phrase "remittance man" has a harsher meaning in Britain, where little sympathy was wasted on a younger son
who—as a loafer, lawbreaker or spendthrift (or all three)—was
expelled from the family hearth. Victorian morality fixed his evils
forever—as if locked in amber and impervious to the forgiveness that
might come with the passage of time. He was gone. Supposedly he
was looking for a good investment his family would help him
purchase. But the family was seldom aware of his suffering or his
painful inadequacy for frontier life. Probably more sympathy was
given him by amused settlers who classed all well-dressed, educated
young gentlemen as remittance men. As a Canadian rancher tren-
chantly observed in the 1890s, "If the definition includes anyone
who has invested money from England in land, then most of the
ranchers in Alberta are remittance men."

No question, a fair proportion of the arrivals were trouble-
makers and/or playboys. Embellished by half-truth, the reasons
for their banishment soon were spread by local gossip. Actually,
England's stiff-necked morality didn't go far on the frontier.
"The reasons some of them were sent away wouldn't provide
more than a few seconds of gossip here in Alberta," said a salty
Canadian observer in the last century.

One common story was that the arriving outcast had lost his sweetheart to another so he left home to become a hermit. Some tales were salacious: "He had an affair with a married woman," or "The upstairs maid had his baby."

Locals also bestowed gratuitous titles, such as Sir or Lord, when in fact few remittance men had them. As younger sons they rarely qualified for a title. But while a good many were simply on a lark, the Canadian rancher noted correctly that a great many had intentions of becoming ranchers with help from home.

But there was another, less obvious, reason for migration—physical defects and disease. It is impossible to overstate the impact on the West of tuberculosis or realize today how deadly it was. While the ugly lesions of smallpox, the gasping of diphtheria victims and the shaking chills of malaria were better known, the quiet killing of the tubercle bacillus surpassed them all. Fever, malaise, coughing and weight loss—these were the symptoms—and then slow death. Poor nutrition and urban crowding fed by the Industrial Revolution made tuberculosis the top killer in the eighteenth and nineteenth centuries.

In his book, *Rocky Mountain Medicine*, Dr. Robert H. Shikes points out that the disease did not spare the countryside or the privileged classes. Victims in England included Keats, Shelley, the Bronte sisters and Elizabeth Barrett Browning. It struck mansions as well as hovels.

Thus, upper class families filled the resorts of Italy, France and Switzerland. A mild climate and open air were believed helpful—and they were. But although the bacterium that causes tuberculosis was discovered in 1882, no single magic bullet emerged as a cure. The boom in health spas continued to expand in the American West. Like Europeans, Americans worshipped at the shrine of a dry climate, and railroads circularized eastern cities with brochures advertising the Western spas, mainly in Colorado. A doctor who had toured Europe proclaimed in the *New York Tribune* that "Colorado Springs is the best resort on the face of the globe for an invalid with lung disease."

Coincidentally, the great outflow of moneyed young Britons for economic reasons occurred at this same time period—the late nineteenth century. Sometimes the motivations were joined.

Ambulatory tuberculosis victims sought opportunity in the West where the health-giving climate would also clear their lungs. For many it worked. But these were hard years: One of every three Coloradans had active tuberculosis and one of every four Coloradans died of it.

The result was that Colorado and neighboring mountain states became the most British of American states, at least for a time. Colorado Springs became Li'l Lunnon, because there were so many Britons among the "lungers" who came to seek the gift of life from the dry, light air at six thousand feet. (As capital city, Denver recognized that the new sanitoria were rivaling its profits as a mining supply center.) Problems emerged as thousands of patients arrived, many of them destitute. Aware that the disease was spread by contagion, the Colorado General Assembly debated—but did not pass—a bill requiring consumptives to wear bells around their necks so healthy citizens could steer a wide berth. Signs discouraging spitting were posted throughout Denver.

Among the British health seekers was a young physician from London, Dr. S. Edwin Solly, who came to Colorado Springs because either he or his wife suffered early symptoms of the disease. Educated at Rugby and the Royal College of Surgeons, he arrived in 1874, when the cause of tuberculosis was unknown. But he realized that the Colorado climate benefited lung suffers, along with good nutrition, hygiene and bed rest. He founded Cragmoor, a sanitarium for the wealthy. But he overcharged his rich patients enough so that for every one hundred paying admissions he could accept fifty indigents. Dr. Solly is a visible example of Britons who came to stay and make substantial contributions to the region's culture, education and progress. There were hundreds of others—educated Easterners as well as Europeans—who came as patients and provided capital and leadership for the Rocky Mountain West.

Tuberculosis wasn't the only ailment that responded to climatic treatment. Isabella L. Bird, plucky daughter of a British clergyman, was prompted to ride horseback through Colorado's Front Range because of fear of an incipient spinal disease diagnosed in Britain. *A Lady's Life in the Rocky Mountains*—a classic book of Western history—was the result, along with a healthy recovery. Did exercise bring her around or was her ailment simply a case of the Victorian vapors that disappeared in the thin mountain air?

Alcoholism wasn't treated as a disease in nineteenth-century Britain. It was regarded as a moral failing. But many a second son found it a chronic companion and solace when his father or older brother sternly urged him to migrate to start a new life as a rancher or plantation owner. With family help, of course. The bottle was endemic to the classic remittance man. Virtually every city in the West had its tales of prodigious drinking by remittance men. Drinking, of course, was a broad social evil in many places outside Britain. At the turn of the century, Sweden launched an intensive, nationwide battle against liquor, as did many nations in the northern latitudes.

Goldwin Smith, retired professor of English history, tells of a remittance man in Ontario. Receiving his monthly check from England, the young man would sprint from the post office to the nearest bar. "I don't know what made them drink," Smith observed. "But there were certainly a lot of them." From the bars of Calgary to Vancouver and south through the Western states to Mexico, the scandal was commonplace—young Britons drinking to stupefaction when their checks arrived.

A wandering remittance man from Denmark whose alcoholic pugnacity earned him the nickname, "the Butting Dane" in northeast Wyoming, Jens Laagard was companionable when sober, but liquor changed him. He would lower his head and charge some putative adversary. His painful butting was tolerated until he went berserk during a chokecherry wine jag and killed a pool hall operator. A rancher invoked frontier justice and killed Laagard with a 30/40 rifle.

Seldom recorded are the genetic and nervous flaws that crippled many a young man's career. The symbolism is probably prehistoric—a crippled member of the tribe was banished, bearing the burden of the tribe's collective evils. Even in historical times physical defects were, in effect, punished. France's greatest statesmen, Charles-Maurice de Talleyrand-Perigord, faced such a reaction. Forced by childhood injury or a congenital clubfoot to give up his claim to the family's title and study for the priesthood, Talleyrand vowed revenge. His bitterness against his parents became the driving force in his pursuit of power.

Disabilities varied widely. The problem for Frank Dickens (mentioned in Chapter 11) was stammering. His famous father, Charles Dickens, regarded hard work as the solution to all problems and insistently gave his younger son elocution lessons and sent him to Germany for further painful studies aimed at preparing Frank to be a doctor. Frank stuttered in German, too, and after failing his medical exams became (with his father's influence) a Northwest Mounted Policeman. Young Frank failed miserably, drank excessively and died at forty-two in 1886.

Some young men were simply inadequate or eccentric, and today might be given counseling. If it hadn't been for his periodic remittances, Charles Cradock, whose English relatives included a famous naval officer, might have vanished without a trace in the wild timber country of northern Colorado. He was an eccentric.

Once, spotting a beautiful team of matched mares hitched to a carriage, Cradock decided he must buy them. Having just put a 500-dollar remittance check in his pocket, Cradock immediately offered that ample sum for the team. The owner loved his horses but the offer was too tempting. He sold. Within a few days Cradock had raced the team from his ranch near Livermore to the city of Fort Collins at such speed that one mare died and the other was permanently crippled.

"Charlie brought on a lot of his troubles," recalls Jack Ogilvy of Boulder, Colorado, himself a son of a Scottish immigrant from a noble family. Ogilvy tells the following story:

> One time Charlie was driving a team and wagon and saw a bear beside the road. He drew out a shotgun and peppered the bear with birdshot—which only made the bear mad. The enraged animal pursued Cradock and his rig down a rough mountain road at top speed and when the bear turned off there was nothing left of the wagon but the tongue and the front axle.

Cradock and his wife were ardent anglers and on one occasion couldn't agree who would fish and who would stay home with their baby. They solved the problem by fastening the child in his high chair in the family kitchen and going fishing together. It happened to be the day some neighboring church ladies, paying an unannounced call, found the untended baby. They were shocked.

Serious disfigurement was a factor in the banishment or self-exile of young men of good families. In the late 1900s, plague had been defeated but other savage contagions persisted and Britons, like other Europeans, still were baffled by the suspicion that a birth defect was hereditary. Like insanity or suicide it was a dark secret to be whispered and kept from the children.

By the time careful writers like John James Fox (1866–1944) described the American West, there was sympathy for the handicapped. At nineteen, this young Briton took a job as a cowboy on a ranch near Rawlins, in the Wyoming Territory. Although he had left school in England at fifteen, Fox continued to educate himself and became a perceptive observer and writer.

His narratives grasped the essential fact that the remittance men he met in the West were merely victims of a social system that turned out nonproductive drones. They faced heavy odds in trying to make a living as miners or ranchers and Fox was a witness to their discontent. Some of his compatriots might believe that remittance men were the unfortunate result of inbreeding among noble families. But Fox knew better. He admired their spunk and met them on friendly terms. If parents were to blame, it was not heredity but family stupidity in sending out an ill-prepared youngster to the frontier.

Some were courageous young men who suffered isolation rather than shame their families. One of Fox's most touching passages concerns a facially scarred young Briton—a victim of lupus—whom he met while visiting a Colorado stockman Dick Brackenbury, who had a ranch on Sand Creek.

Fox knew that Brackenbury and the unnamed Briton had been classmates in Britain and that, because the skin disease had destroyed half the Briton's face, the twenty-five-year-old lad was a self-exile from his genteel family. Still, Fox recorded surprise when they met:

.... when he came into the room to meet me, it was a distinct shock. A beautiful head of wavy brown hair, then the black silk mask, with only one sparkling brown eye to be seen. But he had a strong able body ... and rode daily.

[He had] the most beautiful voice I had ever heard and at some joke of Dick's he broke into a musical laugh. It sounded such a happy laugh, too, that I could scarcely realize that its maker was hiding a horror behind that black silk.

Good old British pluck! I could imagine this fellow as a most lovable companion, son and brother. Yet he had laid out a course for himself in order to make the best of things. [He wanted] to relieve his own family from the depression and embarrassment of his constant presence ... and to escape so far as possible, from being regarded with pity.

And so, out there on Sand Creek, he used to laugh and sing to the banjo, and enjoy taking part in conversation when possible, though he used to take his meals in his own room. Modern surgery could have prevented such a tragedy as his. That seems the pity of it.

A parallel case—but with an upbeat ending—involved a prominent Scottish family—the Haigs. Actually residents of northern England, the Haigs were part of a large clan that produced Haig and Haig whiskey. Among their number was the eminent general, Field Marshal Sir Douglas Haig, who commanded British forces in World War I. Henry Wolseley Haig, a distant cousin of the field marshal, migrated to Nebraska in the 1880s.

Henry Haig was born with a cleft palate, which in the days before modern surgery limited his prospects. With speech capacity reduced, he couldn't pursue the usual course of an educated younger son and become an army officer or minister of the church. As a granddaughter recalls, "Like so many other young Britons there was nothing for him in Britain."

But there was one thing he could do—become an American rancher. His family thus gave him an education and sufficient money to make a modest start as a homesteader in western Nebraska. It wasn't long before his education and intelligence made him a substantial landowner. He wooed and won a waitress in the nearby town of Gering and they had three daughters and a son. The son was educated at private schools and became a Denver surgeon.

Haig built his holdings to a total of eight hundred acres and leased land to tenants, who grew sugar beets, potatoes and other irrigated crops on some of the best land in Scotts Bluff County. Upon his death in 1914, the family was prosperous. The widow and the children continued farming. The name is even on older Nebraska maps. Haig made a deal allowing the Union Pacific Railroad to load livestock at a small yard at the Haig homestead. The result was that his farmstead went on the map as the town of Haig, Nebraska.

Henry, who died at the age of forty-eight, left his mark on the community. His estate totaled 100,000 dollars, which a newspaper obituary said was the largest estate ever filed in Scotts Bluff County to that time. While the Haigs didn't live ostentatiously, their European manners and English-style clothing gave local residents an impression they were nobility. Thus, it is no surprise to find in the Gering Library a historical note by a farm woman that her grandfather once "worked for Lord and Mrs. Henry Haig." Haig was upper class but he had no title except in the eyes of Americans impressed by his family's sophistication.

People who remember Henry Haig's children in the 1920s recall them as projecting a British image. If the Haig girls went horseback riding it was with derby, black coat, riding breeches and boots and—of course—an English saddle. Most of these trappings disappeared in the next generation. A Haig grandson who served in the U.S. Army spent a brief tour of duty in Britain. Did he search out the family seat in northern England? "No," he said, "genealogy doesn't interest me." But like others of his family he got a good education. He later became a petroleum engineer.

Some stories of younger British sons afflicted by personal tragedy have become legends. An example is Clifford Griffin, a boy of delicate health who grew up partly in London, partly at the family's country estate, Brand Hall in Shropshire. The family was large and Clifford and a younger brother, Heneage, were thrown together as playmates and followed similar educational paths—Clifford to Cambridge and Heneage to Oxford. But Clifford was moody and unsure of a career, while Heneage, after a quick look at the clergy, decided on a more active life. After doing the grand tour of the continent—de rigeur for young British gentlemen—Heneage set out for America in the autumn of 1872.

Arriving in Denver—evidently with enough family backing to become an investor in real estate—Heneage Griffin proved adept at making money. He soon had enough resources to make an impact on silver mining at bustling Georgetown, forty miles west of Denver. He purchased and consolidated several properties, the most prosperous of which he called the Seven Thirty Mine (named for the interest rate on his loan). The mine was at an altitude of 10,400 feet and overlooked Georgetown's sister camp, Silver Plume. Finding on a return visit to England that Clifford was still at loose ends and unhappy with life, Heneage persuaded his brother to join him, hoping Colorado would bring him from his doldrums.

This was in 1880 and the mountains seemed to help. Clifford became superintendent of the Seven Thirty and proved competent. But while his brother was a lively, outgoing entrepreneur—on a first-name basis with leading mining men of the region—Clifford was an enigma. There is little on the record, but the mining camp legends have it that Clifford initially joined his brother's active social life in Georgetown on weekends, attended church, went riding and enjoyed mountain adventures. But as years passed he became withdrawn and shunned society, preferring the windswept hillside and his cabin next to the mine. As a musician, Clifford enjoyed playing his violin for visitors. But heavy drinking was taking its toll. On Sunday June 19, 1887, Clifford picked up his English handgun, a .442 John Adams revolver, and shot himself in the head. Maryjoy Martin, a Georgetown writer, noted his passing:

> Somewhere he had lost his dream. He wanted—he knew not what. He needed—but was afraid to ask. He sought—but was terrified to find. ... How long had he carried his disappointments?

Perhaps Heneage knew, because he recalled that Clifford once said he would like to be buried near the mine. Heneage ordered it done and had a ten-foot granite shaft erected over the grave.

Over the next decades—even today—people stopping at Silver Plume or driving by on Interstate 70 tell a different story as they peer skyward at the white shaft visible high on the hill. It is a beautiful story, the kind that spawns legends:

> There was a British remittance man who lived a lonely life as a miner. He had an unhappy love affair in England so he came to Silver Plume to forget. On summer evenings he played his violin for the people down below. One evening his playing was especially beautiful and then they heard a gunshot. Hurrying up to his cabin they found that he had killed himself beside an open grave he had dug so they buried him.

A doubtful story. The strains of a violen would have needed unusually good acoustics to have carried that far. And Clifford killed himself late at night: No one is on record as hearing a shot. Maybe the fatal shot was an accident. But the legend is a fine one and should not be tampered with. Besides, it is so typical of what people believed about remittance men.

The alcoholism does ring true. But was it the product of alienation? The story is fairly typical of the alienation present in the West. Clifford Griffin probably drank to forget something. But as a gentleman he shared few insights with others.

David Williamson, coeditor of *Debrett's Peerage*, offered this view of remittance men as outcasts: "Mostly it was a case of young people being young people. The only difference between then and today is that in those days the things they were sent abroad for were considered to be quite serious offenses."

Of defects like lupus and cleft palates he said, "All these things had no surgical or medical remedies—and it was a time when people were more conscious of them."

So the young Briton suffered in silence. Clifford asked no sympathy for his status as an impoverished gentleman but projected a stiff upper lip that he often buried in drink. Many serious novels were written exploring the mental anguish of this gulf between—and within—classes. Among the most lachrymose was one entitled, *One of a Broken Brigade*, written by Clive Phillipps-Wooley at the turn of the century.

His hero, Noel Johns, loves Pussy Verulane, the beautiful and wealthy English girl with whom he has grown up. But he knows he cannot marry her because his inheritance prospects are nil. So he goes to Canada, seemingly a remittance man, and plunges into drink. When Pussy and Noel's wealthy cousin—who are engaged to be married—come to Canada on a visit, Noel saves his rival from a savage wolf but is killed under the wheels of a speeding train.

Later at the cemetery a woman says to Pussy, "It's no good grieving. There's never any dependence to be placed on those remittance men." But, according to the narrative:

> Pussy did not stay to rebuke the woman. Why should she? She could not know that [Noel] was too proud to be dependent on his own people and that he had [never] taken his allowance from home.

Excellent fodder for Victorian readers. Noel wasn't a remittance man in actual fact but he was one in spirit. Far worse, he was a Victorian gentleman.

❖
_____

"The Whiskey Just Came
in a Steady Flow"

Just about this time I was cooking for four remittance men near
Kindersley [in western Saskatchewan]. I tell you they were quite
a crew. They weren't wanted in England. (Paid to stay in Canada.
Oxford and Cambridge men.)

Oh, my. Let me tell you they lived high. Peaches and cream for
breakfast. We never wanted for nothing. Anything I asked for
cooking they'd get ... it was high, wide and fancy free and if I
wanted a drink why I'd just take one. ... The whisky just came
in a steady flow from Kindersley.

The way they worked it, "my" remittance would run out but
"yours" would be coming in, and when yours was gone then the
other fellow's check would come in. It worked out fine. They
never ran out of money.

Oh, they had homesteads but ... they never did work on them.
Nothing. All they ever did was go out in the bush and bring in
poles and set them up as steeplechase. They all had real good
horses and they'd spend a lot of time jumping. Riding. They rode
to foxes. Except their foxes were coyote ... .

This Chris Murr. He decided he was going to go back to the Old
Country for Christmas. Well, he went back and he said he'd be
gone three or four months. Well, before the end of January he was
back in the shack.

"Well, what happened, Chris? How come you're back so soon?"

"Well," he said, "I'll tell you. We're sitting at breakfast one
morning and I turned my head to say something to my sister

sitting next to me and a maid put a cup of coffee between us and my head hit the coffee and spilled it all over her and I yelled out: 'Jesus Christ!' Well, my mother fainted and my father jumped out of his chair and he ordered me out of the house and when I went back to get my things they ordered me never to come back again. And I got an increase in my remittance."

—Barry Broadfoot
The Pioneer Years

❖

CHAPTER 16

Murder in the Valley of the Second Sons

It was March 30, 1979. Margaret Thatcher was beginning her campaign to become Britain's first woman prime minister. One of her key Tory strategists in the forthcoming May elections was Airey Neave, sixty-three, a colorful soldier, author and military policeman whose aristocratic pedigree masked a tough political intellect. As her chief adviser on Irish affairs, he seemed sure of a cabinet post handling Northern Ireland.

So Neave was much in demand that Friday afternoon as he drove out of the House of Commons garage. He was looking forward to the weekend, but the campaign tactics needed to put the Tories back in power in the May elections were never far from his thoughts.

The hands of Big Ben high overhead signaled that the clock's grating chimes momentarily would boom out the hour of 3:00 P.M. But Airey Neave never heard the sound because the family's history of violence struck first. Or was it a curse?

Any aristocratic family dating from the Norman Conquest has shed much blood, but the Neaves in the nineteenth century recorded an unusual skein of violent death. Unwittingly, Airey Neave was to extend it. Cousins in another Neave branch twelve decades earlier set some kind of a record for dying in bizarre ways and in odd places—and their clock was to strike again.

As he guided his blue Vauxhall automobile onto the ramp of the Commons garage, Neave's life ended in a shattering explosion. Witnesses hurrying to the scene said the vehicle resembled an inflated metallic balloon. Although rescuers recorded Neave's pulse (he was still behind the wheel), he was dead within eight minutes of his arrival at a hospital. Irish Republican Army (IRA) terrorists took credit for attaching the "tilt" bomb to his vehicle—set to explode at the angle of the ramp—but one can't help wondering if the deadly Neave curse wasn't at hand as well. Neave's assassination, of course, wasn't surprising: He had advocated a hard line against the IRA, and the terrorists were taking revenge.

Britain mourned the loss of a good public servant whose tales of escape from a German prison camp had earned him literary acclaim after World War II. He had lived a dangerous life and had hazarded death more than once.

But it was also reminiscent of the strange deaths in the family of a century earlier. One of Neave's collateral ancestors, Sir Richard Digby Neave of Romford, Essex, had six sons by his wife, Mary Arundell. One son died in infancy but the others reached manhood. As was customary, Sir Arundell, the eldest, took the title and the estate. His brothers sought adventure overseas. And they found it—in spades.

Three of them went to India, two with the Army. The youngest of the trio, Wyndham, served as a lieutenant with the seventy-first Highlanders, and was killed putting down the bloody Sepoy Rebellion in 1858. His brother-in-arms, Kenelm Neave, was killed the same year by a tiger according to *The Pueblo Chieftain* (Colorado).

But there was still Reginald, born in 1842 and reared in the quiet atmosphere of an Essex estate. As the youngest surviving son, he seemed almost certain to escape the violence when he chose to seek a business career in Colorado Territory in 1871. He was well mannered and likable. Among his friends was Dr. William Bell, an Englishman and influential official of the Denver & Rio Grande Western Railroad, building west into the mountains from Pueblo. The two men pooled their resources to start a 40,000-dollar cheese factory in Colorado's Wet Mountain Valley, a marvelous scenic paradise that soon would be served by

Bell's new railroad. By 1873, Reginald Neave, then thirty-one, was distributing samples of his cheese to newspapers in the region. Mrs. William Bell, whose splendid mansion today is one of the Colorado Springs' best restaurants, described young Neave in her memoirs and named a girl she said Neave planned to marry.

There was little mystery as to why the Wet Mountain Valley filled up with adventuring young Britons like Neave. One suspects that the English author James Hilton—had he been born earlier—might have placed his mythical Shangri-La in the North American Rockies, an area that appealed to young Britons searching for wilderness enchantment and business opportunity. Many found exactly what they were looking for in the haunting, crystalline beauty of Colorado's Wet Mountain Valley—but they learned that a price was exacted by the rough, lawless land.

This area southwest of Colorado Springs (another British spa) was so appealing to venturesome young British drifters that a local writer labeled it *The Valley of the Second Sons.*

Named for the Wet Mountains bordering it on the east, the long trough of fertile meadowland lies against the spectacular fourteen-thousand-foot Sangre de Cristo range whose granite spikes form a stunning western backdrop for the valley.

The Valley of the Second Sons characterized British settlement this way:

> From Canada, England, Australia and India they came—brilliant, charming, pleasure-seeking young sports, who hunted and fished by day and played the great American game of poker by night. A wild lot intoxicated by freedom, they cast all conventions to the wind, faced danger or privation with a smile, shot up a town in an excess of spirits, herded sheep or cattle, tended their ranches, drank tea at five P.M. and Scotch between times, gave away a hay crop, if they had one, so the harvesting of it would not interfere with pursuit of sport. ... They were the undisputed lords of the realm of freedom.

To young Neave the valley seemed ideal for a cheese factory, but the family curse—dormant for a decade—was on the way. In 1873, another British younger son, Theodore D.B. Pryce, who grew up in the Sussex hamlet of Frant in southeastern England, arrived in Colorado. He had been sent abroad to fend for himself at an early age. His travels are sketchy but he boasted of engaging in knife fights in South America, claiming he once stabbed to death an entire family of seven. When Pryce was imprisoned for murder in Colorado, his admitting officer noted that he had a knife scar over his left eyebrow. He fit the pattern of a remittance man.

But no one in Colorado Territory knew his history when Pryce, twenty-seven, reached the Wet Mountain Valley. He was of middle height, unkempt and unattractive and his educated vocabulary was marred by a nasty disposition. He made few friends in a community rapidly being populated by young men like himself, some to settle down as ranchers or silver miners, others to seek new territory.

Theodore Pryce carried a letter of introduction that he presented to Neave. While most people disliked Pryce, Neave appreciated his educated background and gave him work at the dairy. They often drank whisky together, although Pryce usually indulged to excess. That fatal indulgence prevailed the night of December 14, 1873, when the pair capped a day-long trip to the Huerfano River by joining several other young Britons for drinks at Neave's cheese factory.

An argument arose when Pryce pocketed a clay tobacco pipe belonging to Neave. When the latter recovered it, Pryce said, "Neave, take care. I might lose my temper." A moment later Pryce stepped outside and turned to Neave, saying, "Bring a knife and you shall run me through or I shall run you through."

A witness, Francis Hunter, said that, after Neave joined Pryce outside, "There was a scuffle and it did not last half a minute. Neave brought into the house the knife with which he was stabbed by Pryce." Hunter described the knife as a folding knife with a blade three-and-a-half-inches long. Another witness testified, "Neave said: 'I am stabbed.' As he collapsed Pryce was heard to say, 'I have cut many throats but never killed a friend before.'"

Witnesses testified Pryce then said: "I suppose I shall swing for this."

Which is exactly what frontier justice commonly provided, especially when Colorado newspapers began giving the story lurid treatment. "Murder Most Foul," cried *The Pueblo Chieftain*, adding a subhead, "The Pointed Dagger does its Bloody Work." The *Chieftain* then praised the victim as "generous to a fault" and said the Neave family had "royal standing" in England. Clearly the *Chieftain* favored quick justice.

Pryce easily could have been lynched on the spot had he remained at the cheese factory, near the future site of Westcliffe, Colorado. But early next morning he was taken to Canon City for safekeeping until his trial, set for early May.

Strange things began to happen. The Pryce family was an old one with aristocratic connections. The federal attorney for Colorado, T. E. Alleman, soon complained in Denver that pressures were being applied on Pryce's behalf through the British embassy in Washington. Alleman properly resisted on grounds that the territorial district court in Canon City had jurisdiction.

Pryce had a well-financed defense. The London attorney William Flagg arrived in Colorado and hired Henry M. Teller, a famous future U.S. senator, and Wilbur F. Stone, later a state supreme court justice, to defend his client. But the territory was well equipped, too, with M. H. Thatcher of Pueblo brought in to lead the prosecution.

The trial took only a few days and the judge made short work of claims that Pryce was drunk and didn't know what he was doing. But the justice also cautioned that a hanging verdict could be reached only if Pryce had entertained specific intent to kill Neave, a dubious assumption. He also warned the jurors that "if you believe the evidence that the prisoner said he had cut many throats before, or words to that effect, you will not consider this as proof of the fact or as evidence of the prisoner's guilt. ... Every fact essential to guilt must be proven."

The verdict was guilty and the sentence was life in the penitentiary at Canon City. Fears of lynching were expressed and probably were well founded—a few years later a mob in Canon City took a prisoner from the authorities and hanged him.

But Americans were in awe of British money and power, and Richard A. Bartlett, a historian, decades later concluded, "It seems quite clear that the only thing that saved his [Pryce's] life—for he received life imprisonment—was the awe with which his British background held the local citizens in tow."

Into prison Pryce went. Territorial records are skimpy, reporting only that he died in prison at 5:00 P.M., May 19, 1882, and that his closest relative was his "mother, Dora, of Sussex."

There is, however, a good deal more. The Pryces had never stopped trying to free their kinsman (and later continued seeking the cause of his death). In 1878, after Henry Teller had been elected to the U.S. Senate, a British admiral, William deRohan, made contact with him in Washington. The admiral's request that the case for Pryce's release from prison be laid before Colorado Governor John L. Routt came back negative. Newspaper accounts insist that Pryce starved himself to death, but Pryce's brother in England got word that Pryce was the victim of typhoid fever.

If his death was suicide by starvation, Pryce evidently fell into total despair after state officials rejected his family's attempts to free him. Governor Routt in the 1870s wrote the following letter—apparently extinguishing the last glimmer of hope—to Pryce's mother. The letter of denial follows:

Dora Isabel Pryce
Penns Rocks
North Tunbridge Wells
Sussex

Dear Madam:

I am in receipt of your letter of the 9th. In reply to it, as well as to your former letter, forwarded by the Hon. Robert E. Schenck, U.S. Minister, London, I have to say I have taken special pains to obtain full knowledge of all the facts in reference to the case of your son. After consultation with the presiding judge and one of the attorneys, I can find nothing to extenuate the crime. While sympathizing deeply with your affliction and regretting that I cannot relieve your distress I am compelled to state there is nothing to justify me in setting aside the penalty imposed by the court.

Very respectfully,

John L. Routt, Governor.

In a strange anticlimax to the case, *The Denver Times* in 1903 carried a story reviewing the case and reporting claims from

Britain that Pryce had been freed—at least long enough to claim his share of the family estate. The story involved a sensational British murder case in which Mrs. Florence E. Maybrick, in prison for killing her husband, asked release to appear in court to claim land she owned in the United States. Her attorneys told British courts that Pryce's release from the Colorado prison set a precedent for freeing his client long enough to claim her lands.

In 1916, *The Denver Post*, which didn't begin publication until 1892, reviewed the Pryce case again and made much of its discovery that, as the headline put it, an "Heir to English Title Died in Prison Here." The story was largely speculation: As the younger son of a landed gentleman, Theodore Pryce had no title in prospect.

The *Post* reported other rumors that Pryce had escaped. His death in 1882 is only a single line in the Colorado archives. Since the prison was then under territorial rule the disposal of bodies isn't well documented. Following a recent search, a clerk in the prison's records office noted: "We do have an old cemetery from that period. But the gravestones aren't marked."

The strange story of Theodore Pryce will remain largely shrouded in mystery. Should his grave be located one might suggest that Rudyard Kipling's verse about black sheep be erected in memorium. It seems to cover all the young remittance men pitched out from home too soon:

> We have done with hope and honor,
> We are lost to Love and Truth,
> We are dropping down the ladder rung by rung,
> And the measure of our torment is the measure of our youth,
> God help us, for we knew the worst too soon.

The Perils of Not Drinking

Many Britons—especially remittance men—enjoyed their Scots whisky but some upper class travelers were so snobbishly class conscious that they refused to drink socially with Americans. Such a lordly fellow, accompanied by two servants, stopped for dinner at a stage station in northern Wyoming in the mid-1880s. Cowboys at the bar invited him to have a drink.

The Englishman refused, saying he didn't drink, but soon found a six-shooter pointed at his ear. He quickly changed his mind but protested, "Aw, this American whiskey, I cawn't swallow it, you know."

"Well," said a cowboy. "I'll make a hole in the side of your head so that we can pour it in." He cocked his pistol and the Briton said:

"Aw, that'll do it; I'll drink it." He drank and the cowboys turned to the servants. The same objections cropped up but were quickly muted with a Colt .45. The servants soon were drinking *with* their master—a terrible breach of etiquette. But after a few drinks the Britons managed a bit of strained jollity.

The story, quoted from a Cheyenne newspaper, is from the diary of Edward Marston, an English businessman who in 1885 visited his son, Frank, whom he had located on a ranch near Bozeman, Montana. Marston agreed with the editor's opinion:

The cowboy was wrong in forcing a man to drink, ... But on the other hand snobbishness is not the proper thing in this country, and sensible men generally try, while in Rome, to do as Rome does."

✤

CHAPTER 17

Waiting for the Snipe

As a type, the remittance men seemed to fall into very familiar lines of classification. In many particulars, when you had seen one you'd seen them all. But not completely so. Perhaps the basic line of demarcation would be between the drifting incompetent and the positive rotter.

—*Dr. Gilbert Roe*
"Remittance Men"
Alberta Historical Review, 1954

Expert as he was in Canadian history, Dr. Roe wasn't content with this conclusion so he added:

Their principal function was to bring Englishmen into disrepute. In this they achieved an abounding success. Yet they were often sinned against as well as sinning . . . and deserved sympathy quite as much as blame.

So the picture isn't clear, even today. A major theme of the foregoing chapters is that aristocracy was defensible only as long as society depended on its leadership in providing order through strength of arms and the supervision of peasant labor. British aristocracy won some nineteenth-century breathing room when the terrors of the French Revolution reinforced dependence on the existing class system, even with its admitted failings.

Nevertheless, by the 1870s the aristocracy was doomed as a bastion of power. The next fifty years would see its collapse. Ironically, the world at large saw this trend before the British upper classes did, thanks largely to the remittance man. Arriving overseas as a "drifting incompetent," the remittance man was harbinger of things to come. Hard-eyed frontiersmen saw him as a clown to be cheated largely because of the farcical anachronisms that guided his gentrified upbringing.

The British class system couldn't compete with the world of steam power and modern transport that drew the rural millions from menial, horse-oriented tasks to urban jobs. And while the British gentleman sauntered confidently into the future, his role as a master of an underclass of working people was finished. If he were a younger son, he often sought opportunity abroad.

But it would be a mistake to accept such a judgment without conceding the values of the class system to government, literature, science and social reform. Wealthy families patronized writers and other artists. Leaders in Parliament, in overcoming educational deficiencies and in scientific pioneering, came largely from the patronage of educated gentlemen. Even overseas, Britons made tremendous contributions. Schools were set up to try to overcome British remittance men's ignorance in farming and ranching. The efforts often failed, but the thrust of colonizers and individual migrants brought valuable livestock strains to the overseas grazing ranges. Because there was money to be made, some of the wisest British investments were in railroads and urban development in the undeveloped American and Canadian regions. It is estimated that 500 million dollars in British money was invested in gold and silver mining in the western United States—and even more in Canada.

Surprisingly, even though the book starts its narrative with events that happened more than a century ago, more research is needed into the remittance man's achievements. The reason, says M. Ellen Hughes, a Canadian historian, is that the remittance man's descendants often are ashamed of their forebear's reputation and thus suppress their own history. They should, instead, be proud of their ancestry and its contributions.

In Canada, for example, substantial numbers of young English adventurers joined the Northwest Mounted Police

(NWMP) and later became ranchers (enlistment in the NWMP qualified them for free land when their service ended). M. Ellen Hughes finds that many of these Mounties performed yeoman service keeping the peace in western Canada and curbing the vicious attempts of Americans to smuggle liquor to Canadian Indian tribes.

Even foolish young Britons helped keep real estate moving, often providing the means by which serious farmers were able to sell or buy land at critical times. Bob Edwards, Canadian newspaperman and savage critic of the English, conceded that the remittance man built Calgary and, "without the money he put in circulation Calgary might have withered away on the prairie."

But Hughes, who feels that such contributions have never been quantified, adds, "Because remittance men were considered disreputable, their descendants have tended to downplay ... their family's story. Yet remittance men added greatly to southern Alberta in their contribution of color and humor to the early history of the area." The same is true in Colorado, Kansas, Montana, New Mexico, Texas, Wyoming, the Dakotas and neighboring states.

And, as Bob Edwards would say, they brought money.

But there was a bit of Peter Pan in so many of them that their legacy of foolish innocence will always be a delightful part of their literature. Some of the things they did were incredible, even today.

The Cowichan Valley of Vancouver Island in Canada is an earthly paradise of fruit trees, ranches, rushing streams and beautiful sunsets. The living is easy, and many Britons came here—and still do—to make their modest incomes go as far as possible. It's a tiny bit of England.

One of the valley communities has erected a whimsical bronze tableau of two young men (they could easily be young Englishmen) tricked into hunting snipe. Inspired by youthful innocence, the sculptor has one of his young men kneeling, holding an open-mouthed sack on the forest trail while his companion, beside him, holds aloft a bronze lantern and forever peers into the distance waiting for the snipe some prankster assured them would soon come down the pathway.

The statuary could have been entitled "Remittance Men." The good life these wanderers sought proved all too often to be a will-o'-the-wisp. But failure never dimmed their wonderful sense of humor or their willingness to persevere—as a proper English gentleman should. Many of them grew old and died still waiting for the snipe.

"Snipe Hunt," a sculpture in the Cowichan Valley of British Columbia where many Britions settled, symbolizes futility of the frontier for many young men existing on remittances from home.

❖
_____

Making Marmalade

According to Rudyard Kipling, wherever the Union Jack waved over palm and pine there, also, went marmalade. From the Canadian bush to the Australian outback, the lone outposts of Asia, Africa and other colonial spots came the orders for jars of this sweet, sticky breakfast jam. A breakfast wasn't proper sans marmalade.

But if you were not a moneyed adventurer or a wealthy London businessman on tour you could—horror of horrors— make your own marmalade. Reprinted below is a century-old recipe on how to do it. It comes from the Wet Mountain Valley in Colorado, the area called the Valley of the Second Sons because of the numerous British remittance men who settled there.

The recipe is in the possession of Kay Jensen, whose Scottish grandmother, Gertrude Urquhart, was born in India, grew up in Britain and visited Colorado, where she married Reggie Cusack, an Irishman who ran the Bachelor's Rest lodge for young Britons visiting the valley in the 1890s. Gertrude Urquhart's recipe follows:

> Secure 5 1/2 pounds of fruit, including 3 oranges, 2 grapefruit and 2 lemons. Keep repeating until the weight is right. Slice the fruit extremely thin (one-eighth inch or less) and let stand overnight in 7 qts. of water. Boil until tender and let stand a second night, then add 10 lbs. of sugar. Boil until it jells.
>
> *Note*: quick boiling insures better color. Makes seventeen glasses of marmalade.

Bibliography

Allen, Opal Sweazea. *Narcissa Whitman*. Portland, Oregon: Binfords & Mort, 1959.

Anson, Lady Clodagh. *Victorian Days*. London: Richards Press, 1957.

Athearn, Robert G. *Westward the Briton*. New York: Charles Scribner's Sons, 1953.

Atherton, Lewis. *The Cattle Kings*. Bloomington: Indiana University Press, 1961.

Baillie-Grohman, William A. *Camps in the Rockies—Narrative of Life on the Frontier*. New York: Charles Scribner's Sons, 1905.

Barrymore, Ethel. *Memories: An Autobiography*. New York: Harper & Row, 1955.

Bartlett, Richard A. *The British Remittance Man*. Boulder: University of Colorado Seminar Report, 1949.

Bird, Isabella L. *A Lady's Life in the Rocky Mountains*. London: Virago Press, 1982 (first published 1879).

Botkin, B. A. *A Treasury of Western Folklore*. New York: Crown Publishers, 1951.

Brackenbury, Richard. *The Days of the Open Range*. Cheyenne: Annals of Wyoming, January 1952.

Brado, Edward. *Cattle Kingdom*. Vancouver/Toronto: Douglas & McIntyre, 1964.

Brandt, Ernie. *A Cowboy's Memoirs*. Lethbridge, Alberta: Southern Printing Co. Ltd., 1977.

Broadfoot, Barry. *The Pioneer Years 1895–1914: Memories of Settlers Who Opened the West*. Toronto: Doubleday Ltd., 1976.

Burke's Genealogical and Heraldic History of the Landed Gentry. London: published since 1837.

Burroughs, John R. *Where the Old West Stayed Young*. New York: Bonanza Books, 1962.

Burt, Struthers. *Powder River, Let'er Buck*. New York and Toronto: Farrar & Rinehart, 1938.

Cannadine, David. *The Decline and Fall of the British Aristocracy*. New Haven, Connecticut, and London: Yale University Press, 1990.

Carpenter, Frank G. *Canada and Newfoundland*. New York: Doubleday, Page & Co., 1925.

Cave-Browne-Cave, Sir Genille. *The Cowboy Baronet*. London: Herbert Jenkins Ltd., 1926.

Clay, John. *My Life on the Range*. Chicago, Illinois: Privately printed, 1924.

Craig, John R. *Ranching with Lords and Commons*. Toronto: William Briggs, 1905.

Culley, John H. *Cattle, Horses & Men of the Western Range*. Tucson: University of Arizona Press, 1940.

Cutrer, Thomas. *The English Texans*. San Antonio: University of Texas Institute of Texas Culture. 1985.

Davenport, Odessa, and Porter, Mae Reed. *Scotsman in Buckskin: Sir William Drummond Stewart and the Rocky Mountain Fur Trade*. New York: Hastings House, 1963.

Davis, Lieutenant Britton. *The Truth About Geronimo*. New Haven, Connecticut: Yale University Press, 1929.

Debrett's Peerage, Baronetage and Knightage. London: since 1769.

Digby, Margaret. *Horace Plunkett, an Anglo-American Irishman*. New York: Oxford University Press, 1949.

Downs, Robert B. *Books that Changed America* (Alexis de Tocqueville). London: Macmillan Co., 1970.

Duke, Cordia Sloan and Frantz, Joe B. *6,000 Miles of Fence: Life on the XIT Ranch of Texas*. Austin: University of Texas, 1961.

Dunae, Patrick A. *Gentlemen Emigrants: From the British Public Schools to the Canadian Frontier*. Vancouver/Toronto: Douglas & McIntyre, 1981.

Dunraven, Earl of. *The Great Divide: Travels in the Upper Yellowstone (1874)*. Lincoln: University of Nebraska Press, 1967.

Duthie, Wallace. *The Remittance Man*. Nineteenth Century LVI (November 1899).

Edwards, Bob. *The Best of Bob Edwards*. Edmonton, Alberta: Hartig Publishers, 1975.

Ellis, Anne. *The Life of an Ordinary Woman*. Lincoln: University of Nebraska Press, 1980.

Erickson, Charlotte. *Invisible Immigrants*. Miami: University of Miami Press, 1972.

Feilding, Major General William. *What Shall I Do with My Son?* Nineteenth Century XIII (April 1883).

Fowler, Gene. *Timber Line*. New York: Blue Ribbon Books, 1940.

Fox, John James. *The Far West in the '80s*. Cheyenne: Annals of Wyoming XXI, January 1949.

Frazer, Sir James George. *The Golden Bough*. New York: Macmillan, 1958.

French, Captain William. *Recollections of a Western Ranchman*. Silver City, New Mexico: High-Lonesome Books, 1990 (first published 1928).

Harnack, Curtis. *Gentlemen on the Prairie*. Ames: Iowa State University Press, 1985.

Hendrickson, Gordon Olaf. *Peopling the High Plains*. Cheyenne: Wyoming State Archives and Historical Department, 1977.

Hosokawa, Bill. *Thunder in the Rockies*. New York: William Morrow & Co., 1976.

Howe, Elvon. *Prince Hal Rides the Rockies*. Denver, Colorado: Westerners Brand Book, 1952.

Hughes, Thomas. *Tom Brown's School Days*. New York: Penguin USA, 1949.

Jackson, W. Turrentine. *When Grass Was King: British Interests in the Range Cattle Industry.* Boulder: University of Colorado Press, 1956.

Jarvis, W. H. P. *The Letters of a Remittance Man to His Mother.* Toronto: Musson Book Co., 1909.

Kipling, Rudyard. *Letters to the Family.* Toronto: Macmillan, 1908.

Larson, T. A. *History of Wyoming.* Lincoln: University of Nebraska Press, 1965.

Lavender, David. *The Big Divide.* Garden City, New York: Doubleday & Co., 1948.

Lister, Florence C. and Lister, Robert H. *Chihuahua, Storehouse of Storms.* Albuquerque: University of New Mexico Press, 1966.

Lord, Walter. *A Night to Remember.* New York: Holt, Rinehart & Winston, 1955.

Malcolm, John. *Mortal Ruin.* London: Collins, 1988.

Manchester, William. *The Last Lion: Winston Spencer Churchill.* Boston/Toronto: Little Brown and Co., 1983.

Marcham, Frederick G. *A History of England.* New York: Macmillan Company, 1937.

Marston, Edward. *Frank's Ranche:* London: Sampson, Low, Marston and Searle, 1886.

Martin, MaryJoy. *Suicide Legends, Homicide Rumors: The Griffin Mystery.* Montrose, Colorado: Spes in Deo Publications, 1986.

Merritt, John I. *Baronets and Buffalo.* Missoula, Montana: Mountain Press Publishing Co., 1985.

Michener, James A. "Remittance Man." *Saturday Evening Post* CCXIX, January 1949.

Munro, H. H. *The Short Stories of Saki.* London: John Lane/Bodley Head, 1914.

Nevill, Ralph. *Sporting Days and Sporting Ways.* London: Duckworth & Co., 1910.

Nicol, Eric. *Dickens of the Mounted.* Toronto: McClelland and Stuart, 1990.

Nolan, Frederick W. *The Life and Death of John Henry Tunstall.* Albuquerque: University of New Mexico Press, 1965.

Osgood, Ernest S. *The Day of the Cattleman*. Chicago, Illinois: University of Chicago Press, 1970.

Pelzer, Louis. *The Cattleman's Frontier, 1850–1890*. Glendale, California: The Arthur H. Clark Company.

Pender, Rose. *A Lady's Experiences in the Wild West in 1883*. Lincoln: University of Nebraska Press, 1978.

Phillipps-Wooley, Clive. *One of a Broken Brigade*. London: Smith, Elder, 1897.

Pickle, Joe. *Gettin' Started: Howard County's First 25 Years*. Big Spring, Texas: Heritage Museum, 1980.

Pollock, Frederick. *The Land Laws*. London: Macmillan, 1883.

Porter, Eugene O. *Lord Beresford and Lady Flo*. El Paso: University of Texas at El Paso Press, 1970.

Prebble, John. *The Highland Clearances*. London: Penguin Books, 1969.

Propst, Nell Brown. *The South Platte Trail*. Boulder, Colorado: Pruett Publishing Co., 1979.

Richards, Clarice. "The Valley of the Second Sons". *Colorado Magazine IX*, July 1932.

Rickards, Colin. *Bowler Hats and Stetsons: Stories of Englishmen in the Wild West*. Arlington, Virginia: Potomac Corral of the Westerners, 1990.

Scoville, Orlin. *Remittance Men, Second Sons, and Other Gentlemen of the West*. Arlington, Virginia: Potomac Corral of the Westerners, 1990.

Service, Robert W. *Songs of a Sourdough*. Toronto: William Briggs, 1907.

Shikes, Robert H. *Rocky Mountain Medicine: Doctors, Drugs and Diseases of Early Colorado*. Boulder, Colorado: Johnson Publishing Co., 1986.

Smith, Goldwin. *History of England*. New York: Charles Scribner's Sons, 1957.

Smith, W. Jardine. *Blue-Blooded Boys: An Australian Criticism*. Nineteenth Century XIV, November 1883).

Spence, Clark C. *British Investments and the American Mining Frontier*. Ithaca, New York: Cornell University Press, 1958.

Sprague, Marshall. *Gallery of Dudes*. Lincoln: University of Nebraska Press, 1966.

Sprague, Marshall. *Newport in the Rockies*. Phoenix, Arizona: Sage Press, 1980.

Spring, Agnes Wright. *The Cheyenne Club*. Kansas City, Kansas: Don Ornduff, 1961.

Stone, Lawrence. *Family, Sex and Marriage in England*. New York: Harper & Row, 1977.

Sykes, Christopher Simon. *Black Sheep*. London: Chatto & Windus, 1982.

Taylor, Ralph. *Colorado South of the Border*. Phoenix, Arizona: Sage Books, 1963.

Thomas, Lewis G. *Ranching Period in Southern Alberta*. Calgary: University of Alberta. Master's Thesis, 1935.

Thompson, F.M.L. *English Landed Society in the Nineteenth Century*. London: Routledge & Kegan Paul, 1963.

Turk, Gayle. *Wet Mountain Valley*. Colorado Springs, Colorado: Little London Press, 1975.

Verne, Jules. *Around the World in 80 Days*. New York: Dodd, Mead & Co., 1956.

Von Richthofen, Walter Baron. *Cattle-Raising on the Plains of North America*. Norman: University of Oklahoma Press, 1964.

Wechter, Dixon. *The Saga of American Society*. New York: Charles Scribner's Sons, 1970.

Wilson, Barbara Ker. *Australian Kaleidoscope*. New York: Meredith Press, 1968.

Wilson, C. Anne. *The Book of Marmalade: its Antecedents, its History and its Role in the World Today*. New York: St. Martin's/Marek, 1985.

Woods, Lawrence M. *British Gentlemen in the Wild West*. New York: Macmillan, 1989.

Woods, L. Milton. *Moreton Frewen's Western Adventures*. Laramie: American Heritage Center, University of Wyoming, 1986.

Index